LABOUR BEGINS IN THE MIND

AGNIESZKA PLUTA-SZKARADEK

Lauren, I hope you will enjoy this book as much as I enjoyed 'working' with Agnieseta, author of this book.
Agnieseta was our doula, that we hired or rather invited to Maria's birth, she was our angel and helped us so much during prenatal, labour and postnatal period ♡
Enjoy exploring different ways of labour, that can be magical and beautiful ♥
love xxx Marta

Title: Birth Begins in the Mind

Author: Agnieszka Pluta-Szkaradek

Virtual Assistant: Monika Grzegorzewska, Agnieszka Ciach

Illustrations: Magdalena Bęben

Translation: Marta Klonecka

Cover photo credit: Kinga Taranowska

Collaboration: Olga Barbara Pietrzak, Agnieszka Michalska, Agnieszka Ciach

Second edition 2023

Copyright © 2023 by Agnieszka Pluta-Szkaradek

All rights reserved.

No part of this book may be reproduced in any form or by any electronic or mechanical means, including information storage and retrieval systems, without written permission from the author, except for the use of brief quotations in a book review.

Do you know what it's like when for the past year all you've been able to think about is writing an interesting yet easy to read handbook for future parents, and then suddenly, you realise that you are in fact a walking handbook yourself?

When I realised that this book can't simply just lie alongside all those other typical handbooks, I understood that I have to write this book differently. It had to be written straight from the heart because the journey I've been on changed my life and my way of thinking so much, that I realised that no handbook, not even the best one, could convey what goes on inside a woman's head.

Today I would like to invite you to open up your heart to the things that will happen after you finish reading this book. I want you to experience the beauty of birth and motherhood. Even though at times it's going to be hard and painful, you must remember that it's US, WOMEN, who have been gifted the ability to give birth and the ability to give life. You've had it hidden in you for a long time, and in this book, I am going to help you discover it...**and remember - <u>LABOUR BEGNS IN THE MIND!</u>**

Your doula,
Agnieszka

I open up to welcome my baby

Preface

The author of this book is a woman who is aware of her great, internal power. She's turning to women with LOVE, so that, just like her, they can learn to believe in their **natural power and their abilities to bring life into this world. It is written in their cells, after all.** She desires to change the way that women view labour and show that every healthy woman is capable of giving birth in a beautiful way.

She shares an emotional account of her own birthing experiences; the good and the bad. The **bad** were when she tried to be the **perfect patient** and the perfect breastfeeding mother as per the 'perfect' standards created by various people who tried to give her advice: mothers and aunties who gave birth years ago, acquaintances, and friends with difficult birth experiences. She began to build the **good experiences** when she started to look in herself for answers to questions such as who she really wanted to be in the early stages of her motherhood, as well as when and in what situations she felt happy, safe and loved. She discovered the truth about hormones, emotions, love, and understood the role of contractions and that which the child plays during labour. The child's father was right there beside her during these good experiences. The author wants to highlight just how important it is to have support and mutual understanding when co-parenting. A ground-breaking discovery. She searched deeply in herself and found it, **understanding the relationship that she holds with herself.** Thanks to this:

- she began to trust her body's ability to give birth
- she understood that the baby inside of her feels the same as its mother
- she discovered just what the baby is capable of during birth, and learnt about its needs in the first minutes, days, and weeks after birth

I feel that this book is an extension of my other work, the book 'Urodzić razem i naturalnie'"*. This work took me over a year to perfect and was written to act as an encouragement to drive a change in the Polish labour wards. It was meant to assist women in their journey of finding in themselves the beautiful physiology of labour, without the medical interferences. My book intended to change the surgical approach to childbirth, in which women are treated as objects. I dreamed that the messages I'd hoped to relay in my book would inspire an era of change in the attitudes of new midwives. Now this book, 'Labour Begins in the Mind', has a great opportunity to show midwives and doctors that labour isn't just about the baby's physical transition from the mum's belly and into the outside world. **A new era of compassionate midwifery is coming.**

This book is proof that it's possible to believe in the amazing power of birth which every healthy woman holds, and I hope that women will choose to follow this message.

Dear reader, listen to the author and open your mind to learning about your body and the wisdom that you hold. If you're successful in finding this wisdom, you'll increase the possibility of an amazing birthing experience which will lead to beautiful memories. You'll also allow yourself to enjoy the early stages of motherhood, despite the challenges associated with it.

I would strongly encourage you to look for midwives that are right for you, and to get to know them. They are physiology specialists after all, and it's them who will be leading you through a blessed time in your life: through the birth of your baby and the postpartum stage. Befriend them, teach them about you and your needs, and trust them.

It is crucial that you go see a doctor when your body's behaviour starts to exceed your its physiological limits and when it's necessary to diagnose the cause of these abnormalities so that you can choose an appropriate course of treatment.

Irena Chołuj

A polish midwife with more than fifty years of professional experience, author of the book 'Urodzić razem i naturalnie'.

* The book 'Urodzić razem i naturalnie" is a professional handbook for parents and midwives about giving birth. It focuses on the individuality of the wonderful process of childbirth

Contents

Introduction	11
1. In My Head	17
2. In Your Mind	51
3. In His Mind	76
4. In the Baby's Mind	107
5. In the Older Sibling's Mind	139
6. In Your Mum's, Mother-in-Law's, Grandma's, Auntie's, and Neighbour's Mind	155
7. In the Psychologist's Mind	167
Acknowledgments	185
About the Author	189
Bibliography	191

Introduction

What's the point in reading a book that won't change anything in our lives? What's the point in wasting time on reading when there's a pile of washing waiting to be done? What's the point in reaching for a book when you already know that giving birth is going to be terribly painful, so you might as well just go and book yourself in for a C-section now...

And yet something prompted you to buy this book. Thank you for that. This is your first step in transforming your heart and your mind. This is one of those moments in life after which, once you learn what you are about to learn, things won't be the same. However, you want to just go in and give birth without further preparation, because all women 'somehow' manage to do it one way or another, then maybe this book isn't for you.

But if you don't want to just 'somehow' manage to give birth, and you care for the birth

Introduction

of your baby to be beautiful, conscious, to be filled with the feeling of safety, intimacy, love, and respect for your body, then I would love to welcome you on this journey.

I would also advise you to prepare some tissues because you might find yourself needing to wipe away some tears. They could be happy tears, sad tears, or relatable tears because you might feel that what I'm writing about sounds all too familiar, especially if you've already given birth and, let's face it, it wasn't exactly the most beautiful experience.

So, take a seat in your comfiest chair, snuggle under a cosy blanket, grab a cup of warm tea, and dive into this book. Here, you will find useful information not only for yourself, but also for your partner, your baby, their older siblings (if they happen to have any), and even for your parents and in-laws.

This book is not a handbook. You don't have to do things exactly as I've described them here. It is simply a suggestion to look deeper into yourself and to try find something which women should have been demanding a long time ago: respect for the process of childbirth. Because the way that we come into this world affects not only our future, but also that of the next generation.

My dream is for all future babies to come into this world beautifully, comfortably, peacefully, as well as in their own time. I hope that the new generation will change this world so that it's filled with love, respect, and trust.

Introduction

We won't be able to achieve any of these amazing things without a good birth.

In this book, you will come across many emotions, thoughts and reflections, interesting quotes, and explanations which can all influence the way you feel. Please take into consideration what has happened in my life and allow yourself to emphasise. I didn't write this book for therapeutic purposes, however writing this book has definitely helped me understand certain things, allowing me to feel peace and to finally be able to put away my difficult birthing experiences once and for all. Whilst reading this book, you're going to see how I've changed as a person and I'm going to allow you to see a very intimate and private part of my life... I have a feeling that those tissues we mentioned earlier will come in handy once or twice.

The births I portray in this book vary from one another in many ways: they all take place in different environments, they all take a course of their own, all the pregnancies are led in different countries and with a different means of preparation. You're going to learn a little bit about the history of midwifery, changes in the maternity care system and the approach of midwives to women giving birth. You will see the huge importance of an empathetic midwife who believes in you, cares about the physiological process of the pregnancy and childbirth birth, and who supports you emotionally.

In the first chapter, I will be sharing with you my personal experiences and what happened to me. You'll not only get to know me, but also my family, friends, and my surroundings. I'm going to take you back in time and this will be the chapter in which those tissues might come in handy. I wrote this chapter whilst filled with great inspiration and big realisations, and I can assure you that these words have come straight from my heart. I'll let you in on a secret- I started writing this book all by hand, but once I realised how much rewriting I would have to do, I quickly reached for the help of technology... but that first special copy remains hidden in my magical box of memories which rests upstairs in my loft. Perhaps one day someone will find it, read it, and reach for this copy...

The second chapter, titled 'In Your Mind, will teach you about the physiology of childbirth from the hormonal side of things. I believe that, to have a successful birth, you have to allow your body to do its thing, even if it's doing something you may not have control over. You should know that you can give yourself up to your body, because you will be safe. So, turn off your brain and let your natural instincts take over! In other words, turn off all your rational thoughts and turn on that part of your brain which allowed for the survival of our species for billions of years. Don't be afraid of the pain. Instead, read about its purposes, and let the contractions lead you. Be humble and accept them with love because it is through these good (and effective) contractions that you'll be able to give birth to your baby naturally. Sometimes the main problem of these long and unpleasant births is that the woman unconsciously rejects the contractions and doesn't allow them to take over. This not only makes the birth longer, but also more painful. That's because the contractions aren't effective as they don't produce the desired outcome: namely, lowering the baby in the birthing canal. You'll be able to find out about other interesting facts just like this one in a chapter dedicated especially to YOU, because you are important to me.

Some parts of this book are also dedicated to men, because I believe that they are also essential to the birthing process. Starting from intercourse, during which the sperm joined with the egg cell, to the time of postpartum and the rest of parenthood. Let your man read these parts of the book, so that he feels wanted, needed, and understood.

Introduction

The next chapter is all about the birth of the baby. The way its birth is presented is by no means fictional. It is a reality which you may well find yourself living in. When reading this chapter, make sure you imagine the process of your baby's birth, as well as how your baby will feel. Next, you should compare these feelings to those of your child, as presented in the chapter 'In the Baby's Mind'. This will allow you to better understand and prepare your birth plan.

This book also includes a chapter dedicated to the older siblings. I don't know if you are reading this book whilst pregnant, planning to get pregnant, or if this is your first pregnancy or not. I also don't know if you've got children at home, and if they're also keenly awaiting the arrival of their new baby brother or sister. If you are, however, awaiting the birth of your first child, then I would like you to take a little trip down memory lane back to when you were a child, and I would like you to think about how you were told that you were about to be an older sister.

The 'In the Mind of Your Mum, Mother-in-Law, Grandma, Auntie, and Neighbour' chapter was the one I struggled to write the most. Being assertive and firm whilst also not coming across as rude but being polite is becoming more and more difficult nowadays. Sometimes I feel like we have to fight for absolutely everything, and unfortunately, the word 'fight' makes me think of aggression, violence, as well as physical and mental abuse. In all honesty, I have to say that I wrote this chapter for myself, because I know that I still have lots of work to do when it comes to being assertive, and that I've still got a long road ahead of me.

The last chapter, 'In the Mind of the Psychologist', was written by Agnieszka Michalska. Her different stance on motherhood allowed me to trace back to the memories of my first and second pregnancies. I understood that putting yourself first isn't at all selfish, egoistic, or narcissistic- it is simply healthy. It's like a glass of water that needs to be full. If you are able to give 40%, then your partner and your loved ones give the other 60%. You can be grateful that you even have this glass, yet you're not gonna go very far without the water in it. Doctors say that we are able to survive without food for 40 days, yet without water, that number drops to three... don't let your body, this *motherhood*, go three days without water, otherwise you'll dehydrate yourself.

And now, I would like to wish you all happy reading! I hope your minds get filled with lots of interesting thoughts.

Chapter 1
In My Head

It was a quiet evening. I was led in bed cuddling my eldest daughter. Moments like this, just for the two of us, were becoming less and less common. She used to be my whole world, yet now she had to share the attention with her younger brother and soon with a sister, too. Natalia is an incredibly sensitive little girl. She's smart, creative, joyful, and honest. And, also, not so little anymore. My son was soundly asleep, snuggled into my left leg. Yes, whenever we get the chance to, we sleep together. I felt this great responsibility to shape my daughter's personality. I don't know if this is a good or bad thing, but I can see just how similar she is to me. She has the same twinkle of inspiration in her eyes, you know, the one that gets things done.

Us women are incredibly powerful, you know. But some of us keep that power deeply hidden, overwhelmed by the daily responsibilities that society burdens us with; you 'have to' be the best mother, wife, worker, cook, cleaner, personal driver, psychologist, teacher, best friend, mediator, and God knows who else.

> *That's not true! You don't have to be the best in everything you do, because that's simply just not realistic. All you have to do is live your life in harmony with yourself. You have to discover that power within yourself, listen to your gut, and follow your heart. It's seemingly so simple, yet so difficult to do.*

It was winter. The sun was just about to set. It wasn't snowing like it usually does in England, nor was it raining. Outside my window, it was dry, quiet, and calm. We led cuddling, listening to the beating of our hearts. My dear daughter and I, and my son nestled between my legs. After a while,

Labour Begins in The Mind

Natalia lifted her gaze up to me and asked, **"Mummy, how was I born?"**.

At first, I was confused about the question and thought to myself that that question doesn't make any sense. Ever since she was little, she always used to want to know all about where babies come from. After a while I realised that she wasn't asking about the actual physical birth of a child, because she already knew all about that, but that she wanted to get to know me better. She wanted to get to know my heart.

"Honey," I started to say, as I looked deep into her eyes, searching for a sign that her heart was open to my truth.

"I was 20 years old when you came into my life and changed it forever. You were born in a hospital, in the evening-"

"In a hospital? But why? Were you unwell?", she interrupted.

I continued, "...in the evening, during a snowy winter. **I wasn't ill, baby, I just thought that that was the best and safest way**. Most women in Poland give birth in a hospital, because home births are not reimbursed, and what's worse, they're not all that common."

"*Roomburst* ?? What?"

'Reimbursed. It means that the government doesn't pay midwives to go assist in home births. A woman that wants to give birth at home has to find her own midwife to help her with it and has to pay for it herself."

"Ahh okay, I get it now. But mum, you've already said that before. I wanted to know how I was born."

"Oh", I thought. It's not going to be easy to satisfy the curiosity of an 8-year-old girl.

"Honey, your birth was a good one. Although I didn't know so much about it all back then as I do now, but considering the times, it was a good one. The night before your daddy gave me lots of cuddles, and in the morning when he was going to work, you gave me a little knock from inside the stomach to let me know that you were ready to come out. You were coming out at your own pace until we got to the hospital, although looking back at it now, I think we went there way too soon. I was greeted with a mountain of paperwork to fill out. For the first time in my life, I regretted having two names and a double-barrel surname. I didn't have a birth plan prepared because I didn't know that something like that even existed. We hadn't gone to any birthing classes either because there weren't any in my town. After filling out all that paperwork, I had to have a test done, and then another and another. I spent a lot of time in the shower because the water brought me relief. During one of the many internal exams, I felt very warm and wet, and the synthetic oxytocin slowly creeped from the drip to my blood. I heard that you 'can't go without it'. You see, baby, I really trusted doctors and midwives back then. You're our first child, so nobody ever told me before that there are other ways of giving birth too."

"What about auntie? She works in a hospital…"

"Sweetie, your auntie most often assists in giving women epidurals before a C-section, she's never seen a natural birth before. But I promise you, you will. Will you be my doula[1]? I want to show you that giving birth can be a beautiful experience, filled with respect, peace, and love."

Hearing stories about the births in your family, stories shared on social media, stories passed from one woman to another, information passed from generation to generation, and even your grandma's birthing experiences all shape the way we see birth and the idea we have of it.

If you've only ever been surrounded by hospital stories, ones in which something went wrong and doctors had to intervene, or maybe even ones in which the birth had to end in a c-section, then your subconscious doesn't know that it's possible to give birth differently. On the other hand, if you surround yourself with positive birth stories, and those don't necessarily only have to be home birth stories, but those births in which it's the WOMAN that gives birth, and the people that accompany her support her instead of distracting her, then the subconscious image we have of birth becomes a positive one, and a dream we all have a chance to fulfil. If until now all you've heard about birth has made you think of pain and suffering, with a lack of intimacy and control over your own body, now is your chance to say goodbye to those ideas and start preparing for childbirth all over again.

Imagine that your body knows exactly how it should function. It's time to reset your brain and start from scratch.

IMAGINE *yourself giving birth*

THE FIRST EXERCISE **I would encourage you to try, is imagining yourself giving birth. Such visualization will not only help you familiarise yourself with these**

thoughts, but also helps you organise the values that are important to you when it comes to childbirth.

As you are imagining yourself, pay particular attention to:

Where you are, what you look like, what you're wearing (if anything), who's with you, which position you're in, what your surroundings are (is it your room, or a hospital room? Just generally speaking, imagine your birthing space). Imagine the light, if there's music, and what the temperature in the room is like. You can even try drawing it. It doesn't have to be an artistic masterpiece; it's just about putting your thoughts and what you see before your eyes onto paper.

Labour Begins in The Mind

Task 2

HOW DOES *your partner imagine himself during childbirth?*

ASK your partner to do this exercise. Explain that his task is to draw himself (not you), as a birth companion. You can suggest what he should pay particular attention to (have a look at the suggestions above).

THIS EXERCISE WILL ALLOW you to compare your expectations of what childbirth will look like. It is often the case that men envision it totally differently. Throughout the course of my Polish Birthing School classes, I have noticed that the pictures men draw are exact reflections of the images created by the media: the woman is lying on her back on the hospital bed, with her legs wide apart, hooked up to an ECG monitor and with an IV in her arm.

I believe that going on the birthing journey together will help not only you, but also your partner. You will feel his support and care, and you will both better understand the rights you have. What's more, in return, he will become a true knight, a proud father, and an exceptionally strong man.

A space for your reflections.

Labour Begins in The Mind

AGNIESZKA PLUTA-SZKARADEK

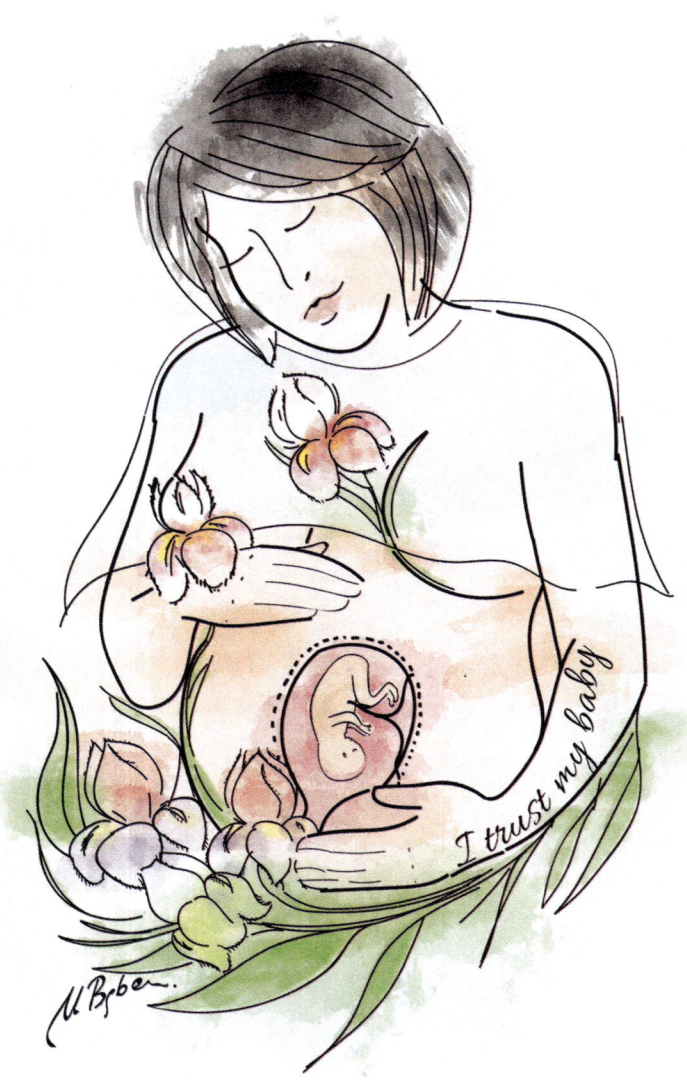

Labour Begins in The Mind

WHEN I FIRST STARTED THINKING ABOUT what I wanted to share in this book with you, I often found myself battling thoughts like "let it go, it's not like you can write anyway", "nobody's going it buy it", or "you'll make a laughingstock of yourself". It was my childhood traumas of constantly having to prove my worth that were coming back to haunt me. And despite my qualifications, experiences and my natural gifts, these thoughts kept coming back... "there's no way you can do it".

And then he came along- my husband Grzesiek. He told me this:

"I believe in you and I will support you to the best of my abilities. **You've dedicated 12 years of our marriage to your family and children**. Go fulfil yourself!"

And lo and behold, my smile returned.

AND SO WE LED THERE, snuggled into each other. Natalia was falling asleep in my arms, and I pondered about what's next. I floated away into my imagination and painted the picture of a beautiful birth. I saw myself swaying my hips, munching on some sweet raspberries, and humming my favourite songs under my breath. Patrycja was making her way down the birthing canal. I held my belly, stroked her, and assured her that everyone was really excited to meet her. I took my time, didn't tense up, and breathed. The air was filled with jasmine, the water in my birthing pool was warm and I was surrounded by people who were important to me; people who understood my journey, although little did they know just how much it would change me.

It was only the 14th week, yet I was already thinking about how our youngest daughter would be born. I had all the details planned out even though I knew that births are unpredictable and like to take a course of their own.

I woke up the next morning to the feeling of my husband planting a sweet kiss on my forehead. I looked into his eyes and knew in my core that I had to tell him…

"Sweetheart, Patrycja will be born at home". I looked deep into his eyes in search of approval. He looked at me and knew that that is exactly what's going to happen and that I won't let anybody take me to the hospital… not after what we went through. Patrycja is our fourth child, so it's fair to say that I know how to give birth by now. There was no need for me to be unnecessarily worried about it at this stage of the pregnancy… **yet I still couldn't help but want to scream "SHE WILL BE BORN AT HOME!"**.

My friends and family were not convinced and constantly tried to get me to change my mind. They asked, "but what if something goes wrong? What if the umbilical cord wraps around her neck? What about this… what about that…?".

No, not this time! They failed to change the beliefs I had about my body or influence the knowledge I had gained in the last four years.

Four years earlier our son Kacper was born, and even though I should be happy that we have a son, my mind is filled with unpleasant memories. **Sadness, regret, despair, hopelessness, humiliation…** these are the words that bounce back like a boomerang every time I think about his birth. And even though I'd rather forget, I still get flooded with flashbacks.

Hospital, delivery room, a stack of paperwork, the midwife and me- still all smiley. If only I had had the perinatal knowledge I have now. If only I had had a midwife who believe in my womanhood. If only I had listened to myself and myself only, and not everyone else around me. A week earlier, when we were doing a hospital viewing, we met the midwife who would later assist in Kacper's birth. She suggested a vaginal examination and then advised the following:

"Friday morning come to the Maternity Assessment Unit at 7am, tell the staff that you have contractions every 3 minutes, pretend a little. You've already had a baby, so I'm sure you know how...".

And so that's what I did. I trusted her and not me or my baby. My baby wasn't ready that day. I was exactly in my 40th week of pregnancy. **It was an entirely induced, medicalised birth, and although it lasted 5 hours, it was the worst experience of my life.** And no, the fact that I had already given birth once did not help at all (surprisingly enough, the first time I gave birth was in the same hospital). **I was stripped of all intimacy, my sense of self-control, and of myself. With every examination, my body was torn into pieces.** Hooked up to an ECG machine, unable to move (because it disturbed the readings), and with no warm showers to ease me, I knew I had made a mistake. But it was already too late. The synthetic oxytocin was already slowly condensing in my bloodstream. No breakfast, no water, no energy... how was I meant to give birth like this? The sight of the delivery suite, the door that was always left wide open, the hospital staff that constantly kept coming in just to do 'something'- **all of this left a mark on me which psychologists and psychiatrists call PTSD, or in other words, Post-Traumatic Stress Disorder**. I had no idea that this is how things would turn out, but, after all, how was I meant to know? And even though I had spent hours preparing for this birth and had even written a birth plan which included all the things I did not want or did not consent to (I watched the midwife tear that plan to pieces), what happened to me that day, was simply traumatic. And it wasn't just the pain or the contractions, (even though they too were much stronger because of the induction),

It's the fact that I wasn't ready.

"Women's strongest feelings, positive and negative, centre on how they have been treated by midwives and doctors."
(A. Kennedy, P. Simkin)
From all the hospital visits I had, the worst one was when my husband had been asked to leave just as I was in the middle of a contraction and a wave of med students came in instead to discuss my case. I tried to just look nice and to keep my cool. And of course, to breath, breath... I still think that they could've waited a minute or two for me to get myself together a little. But a hospital is a hospital; you go in there and give yourself up to the procedures, whether you feel like it or not.

Another downside to giving birth at a hospital is the first encounter you get with your child. I found it hard to enjoy meeting my son because of all the pressure I felt. The constant worrying that I was doing something that was strictly forbidden in the hospital. I didn't know if I could touch or cuddle him, especially after the midwife on duty had seen that Kacper was lying with me and not in the crib and she tried at all costs to convince me that it'd be better for him to lie there and not with me as I was apparently too weak after giving birth. Yes, I was tired, but mentally more than physically. I didn't know how long I could feed him or how long I could do it before someone came to take him away for some more 'necessary' hospital tasks.

The third disadvantage was that I felt very dull, mindless, and tired after such a birth. The total medicalisation of the birth meant that I was still feeling the effect of the drugs even a couple of days after having received them. An upside, however, was that this time around I could sit down without feeling a greater pain, and walking wasn't too problematic either. I was able to give birth without any tears and therefore no sutures were needed. But that was no consolation for me at the time. **Then a few more tearful, lonely nights, a couple more humiliating public examinations, several months of the pain of an injured, broken body and two years of grieving the delivery of my baby.** Going into labour, I knew that I would not consent to an examination with other patients there, and that I would ask to have it done in a separate room. I even said it aloud, but I was silenced with some nonsense excuse and so, forced to look at the lady lying directly across from me, hesitant, I slowly spread my legs. **It was derogatory.... My rightful intimacy taken away from me.**

In the day-to-day life, people see me as a confident, determined, strong and independent woman who knows exactly what she wants. **Yet there, on that maternity ward, I was the 'quiet, obedient little girl' who agreed to everything, all because I let somebody fool me into thinking that doctors know better than the woman in labour herself.** "There is a great difference between a perfect patient and a perfect mother. A perfect patient is obedient, modest and her relationship with medics relies wholly on trust. A perfect mother is strong, wise, brave and is capable of making her own decisions when it comes to the care of her little one. She knows what's best for them. She not only wants to but is also able to be responsible for them. It's not possible to go from one to the other within minutes of giving birth. My take on this is that it is better to decide which one you want to be." (E. Janiuk, E. Lichtenberg-Kokoszka)

Labour Begins in The Mind

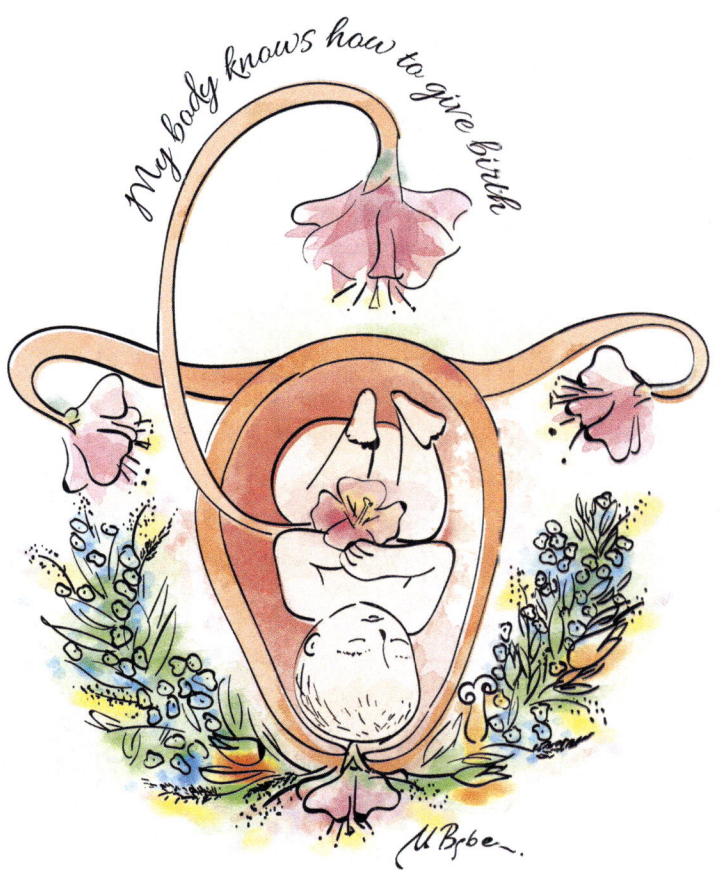

THIS EXPERIENCE HAS BROUGHT me to where I am today and is the reason why you're reading this book right now. I don't want you to experience the avoidable either. You are important to me. Whilst I may not know you personally, I feel a certain bond with you- we are both women, after all. We have more in common than you may think.

After reading this book, I want you to take a good, long look at yourself and find what lies dormant deep within you. I want all the decisions that you make to belong to you and only you, and for you to listen to what your heart tells you. Surround yourself with good people that make you feel happy, free and that bring a million smiles to your face. May you always be yourself and never have to pretend to be someone you who are not.

The society we're living in today sets us the difficult challenge of doing everything perfectly, but as we all know, **THERE'S NO SUCH THING AS A PERFECT PARENT**. Be authentic, be yourself. You are worth more with your faults than you are with your false qualities. And whilst we're on the topic of qualities, consider this one-FEMININITY. There's more to it than you may think.

THE DAYS WERE GOING QUICKLY and eventually we all fell into the routine of everyday life. Each day, my belly was starting to show more and more. I enjoyed every kick, every movement, every heartburn, every nausea. This time I decided to prepare *myself* rather than the baby's room or clothes. I concentrated on building a solid foundation of knowledge. If you want to think about it differently, just think about makeup: it's difficult to have nice, long-lasting makeup without good foundation. I was learning it all… no wait, let me rephrase that- the word 'learning' doesn't work here at all! I was literally absorbing with every millimetre of my body every little piece of information about nature, homebirths, and breastfeeding. And yes, I know what you're thinking: I've not mentioned anything about breastfeeding Kacper. That's simply because there's nothing to tell. I gave up after a month and switched to bottle feeding. I gave up because when you don't receive the right support as a young mother, it is just too difficult. This is especially true when there's an older, demanding daughter at home, too.

As I absorbed all the perinatal knowledge available, I knew I couldn't just leave it all to myself. That would've been unfair, letting other women walk into the lion's den like that. After two years in therapy, I was finally able to lie on my back again without crying. I decided that I was going to do it. **So, I left for Warsaw, completed a training programme, and became a birthing school instructor**. Our family was going through a bit of a crisis at the time, which was mostly caused by my poor mental state.

My relationship with my husband was deteriorating day by day. I blamed not only him but also myself for not being able to be the perfect mother and wife. On the one hand, I could see in him someone that's trying to support me, and on the other, someone completely helpless and powerless in the face of what was happening to us.

The weeks flew past. **Days came and went, and we got used to living together yet apart.** We spent less and less time together and much more time with the children, totally forgetting the foundations to a harmonious family. This went on for a while, and my enthusiasm and thirst for knowledge got brushed aside as my lack of self-confidence and those pesky little thoughts telling me that I'm incapable of anything were taking over.

My heartache kept me from seeing what I really should be doing and kept me from discovering things I would only come to learn many years later. Life's events steered me in the direction of studying pedagogy and I obtained a bachelor's and master's degree in Early Childhood Education. Up until this moment, I had dreamed of working as a teacher with younger kids. Despite sending out many job applications, there was no luck. I sent applications off to primary schools, nurseries, kid's clubs...that was until the idea of starting something of my own came along.

I don't know why, but I always good with kids. At family parties, I was always the one to look after the children. This never bothered me, yet when I became a mum myself, I felt a bit rejected and isolated from the family table. It's not where I was used to sitting. Sometimes I felt like a bit of a clown. **In fact, in our first family company, *ANIMATOR*, I was always the one to play the clown.** We ran all sorts of birthday parties, carnivals, and animations at weddings etc. In an effort to show everyone that I can do things myself and without asking for anybody's help, I often took my daughter to these events. Unfortunately, this quality of mine is still on my 'THINGS TO IMPROVE' list. But these things take time...

And again, we go back to the moment in which Kapi came into our lives; a year later, **we were left with no choice but to**

open our own nursery since there weren't any more spaces in the nearby nurseries. We wanted to work jobs that allowed us to stay close to our kids and tried everything to make our family life work again. But that was only the start of a road filled with many obstacles and problems. We felt the biggest satisfaction when children and their parents were happy with our services, however, after a while, this venture proved unprofitable, and we had to close the business. Yet it's thanks to this enterprise that something else important happened here- I met Karolina. She was a very young, extremely polite and kind midwife who managed to steal my heart within the first 20 seconds of an interview. She's the one who inspired me to change my way of thinking and to start working on myself.

It seems that life had more in store for me than simply just pretending to be a clown or being the manager of a nursery. Full of regret, bitterness, and uncertainty about what would happen tomorrow, with lots of debts and loans, **we decided to move to England**. It was supposed to help us get our life back on track, and maybe even help us return to Poland again one day, too. This year marks five years since we've lived alongside the Queen, and we're doing quite well. Of course, first I had to also deal with an immense feeling of failure, because what do you mean I failed?? Me...*failed*!?

I fought with myself for a long time, blaming laws and regulations, things that I had no real control over. And that's when he came along... or to be more precise, he came over for a coffee- Łukasz, our neighbour from back when we still lived in Poland. He also took the plunge and moved to a place in the UK which was only two hours away from us. It was after his visit that we decided to finally close the whole nursery chapter and to never speak of it again. It's then that I remembered certain words which I once heard in an advert: "You fell over? Get back up! Fix your crown and keep going!". My husband and I spoke for a long time. We both cried, finally getting rid of the last remainders of the sorrow and regret we had both still been feeling. This experience allowed us to open our hearts to our new, shared future of living abroad.

I decided that I want to be a better person, a better wife, and that I want to try for a better life for us, our marriage, and our kids... I really wanted to! I felt that we were already going in the right direction. And so that's how the first four years of our life here in the UK went. But suddenly I realised that none of this matters if I've forgotten about... myself. **I realised that I had stopped trying for what was good for *me*. Overwhelmed by a monotonous day-to-day life, I faded away.** I blended into the mass of all those other women who always drive their kids to school every Monday through to Friday, with no makeup on, dressed in some old jeans and trainers. My only pair of high heels was waiting for an occasion which wasn't coming.

You're probably wondering "okay, but what does this have anything to do with giving birth? Why's she talking about old trainers and school kids...?". Well, let me explain:

> *I am convinced that life can only be complete when all its areas are of equal importance.*

The same principle applies when it comes to giving birth. If you're getting ready for a date with your husband, you're not going to put on your old jeans and a worn-out t-shirt. You want to feel beautiful, feminine, unique, or simply put, sexy! You do your hair, your makeup and you put on those heels which have been patiently waiting in the back of your wardrobe. And so you go on the date, full of enthusiasm and excitement, your oxytocin and endorphin levels rising with every step and every thought that in just a second, it will be just the two of you and nobody else. In just a second, you'll be able to spend time together, you'll cuddle and kiss and touch and sweetly caress each other, all whilst gently whispering 'I love you'. Ahhh, don't mind me just drifting off into a daydream! But let me ask you this: **why do you approach birth with fear? Why are you going into it wearing those old jeans and that worn-out t-shirt?**

I feel safe

Hun, I get it. What I'm asking of you in this book isn't easy... but not impossible either. Get yourself in front of a mirror, look yourself in the eyes, smile, and loudly say: **"HELLO NEW, BEAUTIFUL ME!"**. If this exercise doesn't work the first time around, try it again, day after day, all the way up until the morning of your baby's birth. And after you've finally given birth, go stand in front of that same mirror, all proud and smiley, and thank yourself, because you've just done a hell of a good job.

It was a new day. I needed to understand that when it comes to giving birth, the most important people are me and my baby, that it's me and my body, and that's it our forces combined that will bring the baby into this world. Everybody else is just an aid in this beautiful moment, but I should be looking for strength in myself, and not in the people around me.

At looked at my naked self in the mirror. I no longer saw the little girl who would long for approval everywhere she went. I saw a woman. For the first time, I saw my feminine beauty. Here I am. A woman, a wife, a mother. It's me that gives love to my husband and life to my kids. I am beautiful! I am powerful. I've got the gift of giving life. My body is made to love. My body has been perfectly crafted to bring children into this world. And so, I felt the want to bring another child into this world. We both felt that we could share our love with another child.

It was our tenth wedding anniversary. I blindfolded him, led him to the car and drove him to a hotel. We share some very special moments there, the fruit of which was our second son. We were filled with joy when the pregnancy test revealed two lines.

A few weeks later I started bleeding. I felt that we had lost the baby. After coming back from the doctor, I led weeping on the sofa as the contractions just kept getting stronger and stronger. **He was born. So small, so small that he fit the palm of my hand. I was given the opportunity for that birth to be a home birth too.** Our older children experienced the harshness of life, learning first-hand what they once would've only seen in books and educational films. I think that this was an opportunity to bring us closer together.

It's hard to describe with just a few words what it's like to lose a child. It was a whole mix of emotions which stayed with me for a very long time.

A year later I took part in an event organised by my doula Marysia. It was specifically organised for other parents who have also experienced the loss of a child. It was a time of immense gratitude for my son's short-lived life. At the same time, it also allowed me to close that chapter and put it behind me. Though he will be forever in our hearts and his memory will live forever, because after all, "can a mother forget the baby at her breast and have no compassion on the child she has borne?" (Isaiah 49:15).

After the miscarriage, we only waited one menstrual cycle before we started trying again. To my surprise, it worked the first time around. We ended the last day of the year with some wonderful news: two sharp lines on the pregnancy test. No champagne for me! I was happy, my husband was happy, our children were happy.

Labour Begins in The Mind

AND THIS IS the point in which we return to the start of the book when I told you about my dream to have a homebirth. The due date was fast approaching, and I wondered where the last nine months had gone. It was a hot summer, even by British standards. My due date[2] came and went yet nothing was happening. **I trusted that Pati would come when she was ready.**

She must've been really comfortable there because one week passed, then another, and she was still living inside me. On Friday the 1st of September I was due to have an appointment with my midwife. I went. I felt so amazing that after the appointment we decided to walk home, peacefully making our way around the whole city. It was the first time during the pregnancy that the midwife interfered a little bit, with my consent, and performed a stretch and sweep. She also booked me in for Thursday because the safe time of pregnancy was running out. I was at 42 weeks and three days pregnant.

I woke up to my first contractions at 1am- it was gentle yet distinctive. I knew right away that the birth had started. I tried to sleep a little more but with every contraction, I was overcome with joy. An hour later I called my husband to tell him to come home from work and, in the calmest manner, he replied "you know what, I've got an hour's break now, so I'll just take a quick nap and I'll be right over". I told him that that's cool because he didn't have far from work and there was no way I was going to give birth in the next hour. Grzegorz came home at around three in the morning. I made my way over to the bathtub and the warm water started to ease my contractions... "oh no!", I thought. I didn't want to ease the first phase of labour just as it was all starting. I quickly got out of the tub and, in an effort to keep myself busy, I proceeded to go to the kitchen. Ah yes, the dishes! It just happened that nobody had done them, and we didn't have a dishwasher.

I took out my HOMEBIRTH PLAN and started

colouring and highlighting it before pinning it to the wall. I had planned a dance party to my favourite songs to keep those hips moving but that wasn't about to happen because it was the middle of the night. Grzesiek came in and broke the relative silence by vacuuming the living room (in the middle of the night) and setting up the pool.

I called Marysia to tell her that I'm certain that the birth's started and that she can go ahead and get ready to come over. My doula lived in South London and needed about two and a half hours to get here. She arrived at the train station at 6 am. Grzegorz went to pick her up so that she wouldn't have to struggle up the hill with her six-month-old baby in a baby sling. I was so happy to see her all smiley. I felt inspired by her femininity from the first moment that I met her. I had never met such a natural woman before.

We had breakfast, drank coffee, and talked. All whilst I was giving birth! Actually, let me rephrase that: my body was giving birth and I just went with the flow and let it do its thing. I was giving birth calmly and in my own time, happily welcoming each contraction. They didn't seem all that painful, in fact, they were quite the opposite. Remembering what I had gone through with Kacper, I expected to be knocked off my feet. But that moment never came. The contractions were gentle enough that I was able to get on with my morning relatively normally, sometimes I'd just crouch down for a few seconds. At around 7:30am, I decided to go get some sleep. I hadn't slept since the first contraction, and I was scared that I would be too tired for the beautiful, powerful and strong contractions. And so, I fell hard asleep.

I don't know how long I was asleep for, but indeed I got woken up by a strong and powerful contraction. During the first one, I just led and waited for it to be over. For the second one, I nudged my husband who was lying down next to me. For the third one, I

Labour Begins in The Mind

got up and went to the toilet, "Grzesiek, I have to go poo...". I had no idea that I was already in the active pushing stage of labour.

So, what happened to all those painful contractions that usually come before? Well, there weren't any... not even one. Between the contractions, I ran downstairs to the living room and got into the pool, where I stayed until the end. Marysia took the dog out for a walk. Natalia went with her. Kacper was still fast asleep in his room. **It was all happening so quickly. One contraction after another. Strong, but not painful. Yep, it was definitely the pushing stage! The contractions were so short, that I didn't even have enough time to take a deep breath and try to push.**

And then POP. A pretty distinct sound which can be heard only from the inside. The amniotic sac had ruptured. I felt a contraction and then immediately after I felt the head descend. I touched her whilst she was still inside me.

That's when I discovered that this pain is fascinating to me. It's beautiful. It's justified. It's a good pain because it paves way for a New Life.

Grzesiek called the midwives, but they didn't manage to arrive in time. The head appeared. I felt her go through me. And then her little hand and later the rest of her body came out and floated behind my back. Marysia, who, luckily enough, managed to get home just in time, gave me the baby. I hugged her, my dear daughter. She let out a little cry as she looked around, trying to work out where she was. Natalia was a little sad that she missed her sister being born because she had gone to take her brother upstairs. Apparently, Kacper came downstairs to the living room and stated, "mum, you're interrupting my playtime." I have no recollection of this ever happening. I was definitely in my own little world then... in the world of homebirths.

Natalia threw some rose petals into the pool and put a little headband on her sister's head. We took a couple of photos to have a little memento. Ladies, don't forget to put on your best waterproof mascara for your water birth... the first photo I have with my baby could probably be titled 'Mama Panda cuddling her little one'.

The midwives came just as we were getting out of the pool. I didn't plan for a freebirth[3], but I am extremely grateful for how it went. I held Patrycja close to me as I waited for the placenta to be born. I don't really know how long it took, but I don't think it took very long. When we were completely sure that the umbilical cord was white and had stopped pulsating, Natalia proudly cut it. Our son watched everything from a safe distance. Before the birth, we had asked our children many times if they wanted to be home for it or if would rather go to auntie Dorota's house. They wanted to stay. We would have respected whatever choice they would have made, because it was an extraordinary experience for the whole family.

I felt responsible for the picture of birth that I was painting for my daughter, who will one day hopefully have children of her own, but also for my son, who will one day hopefully become a father.

We rested on the sofa for a few hours. I felt well, and the levels of endorphins and oxytocin made me feel like I was ready to go to a birthing party at the play port. Of course, it was Grzegorz that took the kids there, whilst I slept at home, cuddling Patrycja.

Later that evening, a crowd of people showed up at our house. It was the members of the choir we sang in during Sunday Mass. **I felt better than ever before.**

I was bursting with pride. I knew that from now on, my life would no longer feel like there's something missing. It was now complete.

Giving birth at home brought out in me a strength, courage, bravery, and power that was hidden deep inside me.

The greatest gift that I have ever received was being able to experience birth in its purest, most natural form. If I hadn't experienced it, I wouldn't be sat here writing to you right now. And my husband, who was my birthing companion, understood that "you can't actively help a woman give birth. The aim is to avoid unnecessarily disturbing her". (M. Odent).

Now you know the journey that I went through to get to where I am today. The day of Patrycja's birth is also the day when I celebrate me- A NEW WOMAN. I can't say that that day I was born as a mother, because I already was one. Instead, **I was reborn as a woman.**

This new femininity of mine is not about makeup, dresses, or stilettos (although even those I now wear more often). This femininity is all about believing that we are made for this.

Each one of us, and you too, can give birth to a child in the most beautiful way imaginable.

The last part of my perfect little plan was to get myself a qualification which would allow me to work as a doula. I did that as fast as I could. As soon as the opportunity came up, I didn't hesitate for even a second.

AGNIESZKA PLUTA-SZKARADEK

And I'm all for you now. If you need me, I'll be there.

A space for your reflections.

Labour Begins in The Mind

---

1. A doula, most simply put, is a non-medical midwife who supports the woman and her partner throughout the pregnancy, birth, and the postpartum period.

The doula's experiences and knowledge can allow for an easier birthing experience. A doula supports the mother emotionally, encouraging her and giving her strength. Doulas also encourage active childbirth. Doulas massage, hold, and care for the safety and intimacy of a woman in labour. A doula is experienced in her own motherhood and has the relevant qualifications which allow her to perform this job. A doula is like a 'birthing bestie'.
2. I use the words 'due date' figuratively here because due date is quite a broad concept. When I used the words 'due date' I actually mean the very middle of it, or in other words, the 40th week of pregnancy.
3. A freebirth is birth without any medical or midwifery assistance.

Chapter 2
In Your Mind

When I first realised that I cannot remain indifferent to what had happened to me and to the changes that had taken place in my mind, I understood that I had to do something about it. I had to act. But how was I going to do that? First, I completed my training to become a birthing school instructor, and a few years later, I completed another training which allowed me to become a doula. I'm continuing to expand my knowledge because I think that it's never too late to learn.

Now it's time for there to be peace in your mind, too, and I will try to make sure that this peace comes, and that you feel safe. I hope that your birth is an experience that strengthens you in every way...

Physically, because your body knows how to give birth; emotionally, because you are safe during the birth; spiritually, because you are the goddess of this birth; as well as mentally, because it is you who is giving birth, and not your husband, midwife, or your doula.

You are important to me! You are a woman who is made to bring life into this world. Notice how, as Marie Mongan writes, "when you change the way you perceive childbirth, the way you give birth will also change".

The starting point to changing the way in which you think is all about realizing just how humanity has managed to survive all this time. Dating all the way back to Adam and Eve (or Lucy- each to their own), women gave birth naturally. They never took birthing classes; they adopted intuitive positions and made the sounds their body told them to make. And it worked! And now? Now we're living in a time where natural births are seen as a peculiarity, and a homebirth is seen as something 'completely crazy' and reserved only for hippies. Whatever happened to our innate abilities to give birth? They got taken away from us! A part of our femininity has been savagely taken away from us.

In Poland, it was all well and good right up until the Second World War broke out. Women gave birth at home with the help of midwives, *babki*[4] (the doulas of that time), and other women. Men were often asked to leave the room so they could let the women concentrate. You probably already know why they asked men to go boil a big pot of water...to keep them busy. And what did the politicians do? After the war, they reshaped the national health system and set up the healthcare insurance funds, yet this was not enough for them. In the 60s, they introduced hospital births in order to deprive women of their dignity, respect and their right to choose. From then on, pinned to beds, deprived of intimacy, naked, with their legs spread out to the side and tied, they gave birth in pain, without food water or the ability to move freely.

[4]*Babki were skilled older women who lived in the villages and helped other women give birth. They were often untrained but very experienced.*

How are you meant to give birth in such conditions? The situation described above is already bad enough, and then what about the feelings, emotions, and mental state of these women? It is not surprising then, why we've heard so many birth horror stories from those times. Even I would've been absolutely terrified of giving birth, having heard such stories from my mother, grandmother, or aunt. Maybe that's why my mother never talked to me about it. Maybe she's stuck feeling like she's lost something important? I don't know, I've never asked... and I think I'll leave it that way so that I don't bring things up from the past. Those births were completely medicalised, and women were treated like experimental bunnies. They were given opiates which dumbed them out so much that didn't even remember the whole labour. This also impacted their milk production and thus breastfeeding, too. And you might have realised already that it was a time in history when the pharmaceutical industry was booming, and they started mass producing formula milks. If you really were to sit down and properly think about it, you can easily spot a correlation between the rising number of medicalised births and bottle-feeding. I was also bottle-fed. Apparently, I didn't want to drink the milk. However, I suspect that my mum simply didn't get the right help and support necessary and just gave up. At six weeks old, I was already eating chicken soup... yes, really!

And that's why I care so much about you, the things that go on inside your head, and the way that you perceive birth. Let me say it again: I care about your perception.

You're probably reading this because you're pregnant, or you already were, and now you're expecting again. **I want you to not feel bad about yourself, and for you to see your child as a great miracle**. "You're not alone nor will you ever be again. Not only is there another human being living inside of you but there's also another heart beating inside of you" (M. Knedler).

Stop for a second, breathe deeply and slowly, get yourself a cup of hot tea, go sit comfortably in your favourite spot, snuggle into a cosy blanket, and immerse yourself in this book. I'm going to guide you through the physiological process of birth, looking at it more from a spiritual side of things, rather than the medical side, which you can easily find lots of information about on the internet.

I've said it a few times already, but I'll say it again: "birth is a physiological process, which each future mother has to go through and can go through. It's a process balanced between beauty and danger. It must be understood that you can welcome a child into this world, but you could also lose it or die yourself. Nature doesn't always guarantee a happy ending. By saying yes to life, we are also saying yes to death. You cannot separate birth from death" (M. Knedler). These are words from the book *Położna z Auschwitz*. They are not meant to be enough but are just meant to be a thinking point. It's just the way life goes. It's good to be born well, live beautifully and to die with respect and dignity, knowing that you've lived life to the fullest.

To me, the way in which my children come into this world and in what kind of environment is very important. The way they decide to live their lives is up to them, especially when they grow up, but the way in which they are born is up to me. Knowing what natural births look like allows me to make decisions with the awareness that life is too short to worry about the silly, little things. Following on from the Auschwitz midwife, Stanisława Leszczyńska, nature knows what it's doing.

In the previous chapter, 'In My Mind', I told you about my miscarriage. It was a difficult experience, but equally very strengthening. Sometimes we have no control over certain things and that's just the way it must be. But there are also many things which we do have control over.

"When a woman chooses to become a mother, she agrees to constantly learn new things and to discover all the things associated with this role" (L. Dillow). Whilst you're preparing yourself for birth, you're also preparing yourself to become a mother. And it doesn't matter if this is your first, second or fifth birth. Each time, you're learning how to be the mother to the child you're carrying under your heart. **Each pregnancy is different because your womb holds a different baby**. Each birth is different because there is a new human coming into this world. A new, individual human, who has their own personality, and a unique DNA.

Women often have all sorts of negative thoughts about the birth, pregnancy, and motherhood... "what if I won't be able to do it?", "it's definitely going to hurt", "I think I'd rather just go straight for a c-section...", "what if there are complications??".

Ahh, complications. Do you know what they usually stem from? They mainly arise when the hormones responsible for the birth process get disrupted or inhibited. These hormones responsible are oxytocin, endorphins, adrenaline, and prolactin. I'll try to explain them to you as simply as I can.

Oxytocin

OXYTOCIN IS PRODUCED by the pituitary gland during intimate moments: when you're making love with your husband, when you're cuddling, when you're kissing...

Natural oxytocin is a hormone which nature has blessed us with to ease the birthing process for each one of us.

Oxytocin is often called the hormone of love because it is produced by our body whenever we feel loved, safe, respected, and accepted. It is therefore secreted during sexual encounters when you're cuddling, kissing, or caressing each other, but also during childbirth and when you're breastfeeding,

It was there when you conceived your child, and I bet that no one told you guys how to do it, nor did they interrupt, examine, or monitor you. And so? Did it work? Yes it did because you're pregnant! You've got this great gift within you; you just need to fully discover it.

Oxytocin loves the following three things: QUIETNESS, DARKNESS, and WARMTH. The thing that's amazing, is that it's present both in you and in your partner. You both get flooded with waves of oxytocin and the accompanying endorphins.

Labour Begins in The Mind

Think about the last time you felt happy, loved, or safe. How did your body react? Was it tense? I'm sure that it was quite the opposite. That's exactly why our bodies produce oxytocin during birth. It would be a lot harder for tense muscles to adjust to the tempo and rhythm of the birthing process, and that would only make it harder for the baby to enter the birthing canal.

When you're giving birth, make your mind do a little work and try to think of something positive. You can imagine absolutely anything you want, as long as it relaxes your body. In your imagination, you can kiss, hug, reminisce about places or things that bring you together and fuel your love.

Every couple has some positive memories. Go take a trip down memory lane. What about the first time you met? Your first date and the butterflies you felt? What about your honeymoon or walks along the beach in the moonlight? You yourself know best what makes you feel like you're in paradise. Why not play your favourite song, or spray a favourite scent that brings sweet memories to your mind? This way, you will pave the way for a successful birth.

Oxytocin is responsible for the function of uterine contractions. "A contraction is a tool for bringing a baby into the world and you should use it wisely. Your senses will guide you through it. The pain in childbirth comes from physiology and it is a result of a contraction, without which you will not be able to deliver your baby". (I. Dembinska)

Oxytocin is a hormone which nature has blessed us with to ensure that births run smoothly so that every woman can cope with them. **As you already know, oxytocin is released gradually, and this helps contractions gently increase in strength.**

As soon as you give a woman an IV with synthetic oxytocin,

her body stops producing it naturally, and, consequently, the contractions become much stronger and much more frequent. What's more, synthetic oxytocin also blocks the production of the remaining hormones: endorphin, adrenaline, and prolactin. And do you know what the consequences are? Your uterus starts going crazy, driven by the droplets of synthetic fluid, and your brain (i.e. the mind), does not know about any of this and thus cannot cooperate. Hence the inspiration for the title of the booking you are currently sat reading.

> *We actually give birth with our head and mind, and the abdomen and uterus are just the tools for making it happen.*

Synthetic oxytocin cannot cross the blood-brain barrier, meaning that it can't be transferred from the body to the brain, making it unable to fulfil the role of the 'love hormone'.

When a woman gets given synthetic oxytocin, she gets flooded with waves of contractions coming in one after the other, and the gap between them is shorter, and sometimes even non-existent, than it would be with naturally induced contractions. This means that the uterus gets overstimulated. Administering a high dose of synthetic oxytocin causes an overstimulation (hyperstimulation), which can deprive the child of the necessary blood and oxygen supply, and this can cause a dysfunction of their heart. All of this runs the risk of risking the life of the child or even the rupture the uterus. Consequently, such birth often ends in a caesarean section.

Women who have been administered synthetic oxytocin are at risk of significant bleeding after birth. This is because the uterus loses oxytocin receptors and thus does not respond to the natural peak level of oxytocin that occurs after childbirth and prevents bleeding.

Labour Begins in The Mind

My body is designed to birth naturally

ENDORPHINS

As well as natural oxytocin, your body's endorphin levels also rise. **Simply put, endorphins are 'natural drugs' which help make births more manageable for women**. But for them to work, you need to understand their significance…

Endorphins resemble opiates in their structure, and so **they act as a natural anaesthetic during childbirth.** So, what can you do to benefit from these endorphins? **First and foremost, you need to understand the role of labour contractions, enjoy each incoming wave, and aim to make your contractions longer, stronger, and more frequent.** This may seem a little unusual, given that normally our first reaction to pain is tensing our muscles and trying to escape the pain as quickly as possible. Yet here I am, convincing you to change your way of thinking so that you concentrate on having as many of these contractions as possible. I know how hard it is in practice, when your whole body starts to shake, all your rational thoughts leave your mind, your stomach (or spine) feels like it's getting torn from the inside out, and to make matters worse, you're feeling this pressure in your crotch, which makes it feel like the baby's about to fall out…

But without these endorphins, it really is hard to have a good delivery and make fond memories. The level of endorphins peaks the moment we see our baby for the first time. Their sudden and powerful ejection makes us forget all that pain, and we begin to rejoice in the baby we can now hold close to our chests. For you to experience these endorphins in your body, you need to be able to feel safe during your birth. Less important here is the place you give birth because even in a hospital you can feel this way.

However, I believe that women tend to feel a lot more comfortable at home, and that the levels of the oxytocin and adrenaline produced are much higher.

Yet what's most important to me is how you feel. I still wish for this book to be a chance for you to discover yourself all over again. Even if there's not much time left now until your due date, I know that you know how to give birth and that you can do it. "All you have to do is believe and listen to your body. You have to think of this child that's paving its way into this world and hope that this world is worth living in". (M. Knedler)

"What's useful in labour is the realisation that you are working together as a team with your child. The child is an equally active participant in this birth, just like you, and they also need the faith and support of a birth companion." (I. Dembińska)

And so, **it's you who gets to decide how you are going to bring your child into this world**. By learning about the physiology of the female body and childbirth, you're well on your way to the beautiful journey that is childbirth.

Another important factor is your due date. The middle, or 40th week of pregnancy, is assumed as the standard, but the term 'due date' actually defines a baby born between the 37th week and the 42nd week of pregnancy because the pregnancy is considered to be full-term from the 37th week. As you can see, this range is huge, as it is as much as six weeks. Comparing women's due dates is like comparing different types of trees. Each one of you ladies reading this book will give birth when the time comes, just like every tree blooms when it's their time.

Waiting anxiously for the baby or, worse yet, the doctors scaring you with an induction because 'you're past your due date' (wow, it's barely the 41st week!), immensely increases the adrenaline production in your body, even though its place during labour should only be brief. It's best if the production doesn't start at the end of the pregnancy or in the first phase of labour.

ADRENALINE

Ah yes, so what's the deal with this whole adrenaline thing anyway? Is it good or not? **This hormone, which is secreted by the adrenal gland, is considered rather disruptive during labour, and is only useful when the baby starts coming out.** During childbirth, the cervical dilation stage is significantly longer than the active pushing stage. Consequently, adrenaline is not needed and its release during the first stage of labour can stop the labour for several hours. If we have less patient hospital staff looking after us, then you will find the words 'failure to progress' written in your documents, which will cause a whole load of interventions and medicalisations, including the risk of a c-section.

Let's also not forget that when the baby's head starts coming out, mothers need an extra top up of strength, power and energy because this is the toughest and most tiring part of the whole birthing process. If you can feel what we tend to call the 'fire ring'[1], then you know that the baby's head is well on its way out. **This is why during the second stage of labour, the adrenaline rushes in- to energise you and minimise the feeling of pain when the baby's head passes through your vagina.** Just a little more and will having a beautiful, long-awaited baby lying snuggled into your chest. Your adrenaline levels drop rapidly, making room for the oxytocin, endorphins, and prolactin, which is also about to kick into action.

##

Prolactin, as its name wonderfully already suggests (pro= for, lactin=lactation), is **the hormone responsible for the production of breast milk**. The level of prolactin gradually increases throughout the pregnancy, but significantly falls during the actual labour. **It's not until the very end, when the placenta gets delivered, that the prolactin kicks back in**. The way it happens is amazing; in an instant there becomes a lot of it, and it becomes responsible for the most important job yet- breastfeeding.

Prolactin also heavily influences the way we act and feel; **it's thanks to this hormone that a young mother takes care of her newborn and is ready to protect it like a true lioness, putting the baby's needs above her own**. Having high levels of this hormone is what causes women to have a **nearly non-existent libido.** Prolactin inhibits the production of oestrogen, lowering her sexual needs, which allows her to care for her newly born baby better. You should probably let your partner know about this, so that he doesn't feel rejected. Make sure he knows that you still love him very much and need him.

Knowing that you've made it so far in this book and that you've read so many of my words makes me so happy. I feel like the things I want to convey to help prepare you for labour are flowing straight from my heart an onto these pages. This topic is so close to my heart, that sometimes I forget that there are people out there who may look at these things from a different perspective and understand things completely differently.

Accepting our femininity and all that happens to our body from the moment we have our first period heavily influences how we perceive childbirth. When we get period pains, it's our body telling us to "do a little something for yourself, rest, and slow down". The way I see it, there are two types of pain we experience during labour: the physical one and the mental one. I think every little girl wonders at least once what it's like to give birth. It's good when our mums portray birth to us in a positive way. Similarly, our own experiences also influence what we will one day tell our daughters (and sons) about childbirth.

From everything that I've just told you about hormones, we can draw only one conclusion: that labour truly does begin in the mind, whether we want it or not. Isn't our brain a wonderful little thing?

Labour Begins in The Mind

I give birth in agreement with myself

Is what you've learnt so far enough for you? My guess is that it's not. And very well because I could talk and write about birth for hours on end. No, but really! **I would never have thought that there would ever come a time when I would feel an immense and heart-filling happiness and fulfilment at the thought of childbirth.** I hope that your memories bring you an equal amount of joy. That's why I'm so happy that you're still here with me.

You've managed to get through the most important part of the book- the one that's all about how hormones work. It is thanks to them that any of this even happens. Understanding just how at one we are with our womanhood, and how closely it all interconnects, allows us to believe and trust that our bodies are simply perfectly made to give birth to children and our breasts are simply perfectly made to feed. Yes, breasts- or in other words the mammary gland- are not first and foremost something erotic. They only become so at the end of the 20th Century with the rise of feminism, which peaked all the way back in the First World War. And since we're talking about boobs...

How do you see your breasts? Do you like them? Do you like to touch them? There's a reason why I'm asking these questions. Breastfeeding is wonderful period in your life for many reasons. On the one hand, it's a time when there'll be lots of tears, sometimes a little bit of pain, but also happy tears. On the other hand, it is also a time when our breasts are exposed to the public eye, tugging, biting, milk stasis, and inflammation amongst many other things. Today, however, I'm not going to be talking too much about breastfeeding. That's because when I started writing this book, I became flooded with lots of other interesting ideas, one of them being perhaps a second part to this book. How about 'Breastfeeding Begins in the Mind'? We'll see. If it all goes well, then maybe I'll develop this topic further another time.

Don't forget that you can always make good use of my support through a lactation class or an online workshop on www.polskaszkolarodzenia.co.uk Eh, why not throw in a little ad midbook?

Anyways, let's get back to childbirth and its physiology. You already know that the whole process is led by hormones and it's thanks to them that it goes smoothly enough for each one of us to be able to rise to its challenge. If it wasn't this way, humanity wouldn't have been able to survive for this long. Indeed, it seems that "women's bodies have to be pretty awesome, otherwise there wouldn't be so many people on this planet" (I.M. Gaskin).

My biggest dream is that one day births get treated as a natural event that only sometimes require medical support, and not as a medical event that only sometimes happens naturally. When you allow your baby to be independent, the labour will gain a totally different dimension. You don't push the baby out by force, instead you let the baby be born at its own pace. It's the baby who this important task belongs to; it must get out into this world on its own, so that from that moment on, it's able to breathe on its own, feed on its own and live.

Irena Chołuj writes that "when you feel the contractions, you are being called to interact and work with your body, and to submit yourself to the activity as directed by your body". Throughout my work, I sometimes find myself trying to convince women that childbirth is first and foremost an emotional event, one that stays with the woman forever. It is also a psychological event because it's mainly the head that does the majority of the work.

Postpartum disorders are most often caused by the lack of safety or intimacy during the pregnancy or childbirth.

These postpartum disorders affect our mood in the first few weeks after childbirth and **can lead to more serious complications, such as Post Traumatic Stress Disorder (PTSD) or postpartum depression.** That's why I dare say that the path you take on your journey to becoming a mother is an extremely important one.

The women who have worked with me in preparation for this big day have noticed a big difference in the way they perceive childbirth. A lot of them have said that they never imagined that they could ever see birth differently than the way that they've been shown in the media, namely, as something bad and extremely painful. And then there's also that surprised look on the face of all the men when they find out that it's possible to give birth in different ways to the ones they've seen shown. I would say that about 80% of all the men who have attended classes at the Polska Szkoła Rodzenia w UK (Polish Birthing School in the UK), associated birth with the typical 'dead frog' pose, or what we can also refer to as 'the stranded beetle position'. That's why it is so important to be in a position that's comfortable and appropriate to you when giving birth, and not to the doctor or the midwife.

The French midwife Michel Odent often says that "to improve obstetric care (...) it's necessary to give childbirth back to women". It is the woman who is the main character in this scenario. It is her preparation, commitment and mindset that determines the course of the birth.

Please, take a deep look at yourself. Find your inner self and give her a tight hug. Make it a friendly one and put a smile on her face. You are important. At every stage of your life, you are important. You are special. There's nobody else out there quite like you. I am so happy that you're here and that I can accompany you on your journey to motherhood. Your needs are my needs because I feel an incredible connection with you. We are both women. We are both wives. We are both mothers.

When women are close to their due date, they often come across this big urge to organise and prepare everything, and to make sure they've dotted all the i's and crossed all the t's. That's called nesting. Make sure that your nest is all warm, cosy, safe, nice, and comfortable. You will spend your postpartum in there, and during that time, your main task will be to rest. Yes, I'm aware how that sounds... rest? With a newborn?! But indeed, it is possible. It's possible to enjoy your shared moments together, it's just that it will be a little hard for you physically.

AGNIESZKA PLUTA-SZKARADEK

Labour Begins in The Mind

THE WOMAN KNOWS EXACTLY what to do for the birth to go smoothly. It's important for her to simply just be herself. If something hurts, try to find a position and a solution that will ease this pain. The position you decide to take will be the best one for you and your baby.

Michel Odent once wrote "to change the world, we must first change the way the babies are being born".

By blindly following all that comes with this modern present-day life, we lose our natural instincts. We forget all that our bodies and minds are capable of. Or maybe it's that we don't want to know how much we're truly capable of? Maybe putting births in the hands of the doctors and their loyalty to medicine makes us feel excused when something goes wrong because it's easy to put the blame on something we have no control over, so long as we don't feel responsible.

When complications arise, it's common to hear women blaming external factors: "it's so great that I had a c-section because the baby was big", "they saved my baby, it was getting hypoxia", "I don't know how I would've managed without the forceps", "it's so good that the midwife didn't let me eat because I had to have an emergency caesarean". **In fact, the cause of these complications lies elsewhere- it starts in our minds.**

If we are afraid, we hold the baby back from coming out and into this world. Our body physically blocks itself from giving birth, the labour gets prolonged, and we get weaker and more tired.

What's also important is where you give birth and the way in which it gets carried out. If, for example, the birth is a strictly medicalised one, you're pretty much guaranteed to end up with that typical birth horror story you'd find on one of those mum groups on Facebook. **And I really don't want you to join all those women who, at the very thought of giving birth again, begin shaking with fear**. Instead, you could take care of yourself. Whilst you're pregnant, you have all the time to get on top of your reading, to do research, gain information, to surround yourself with good people and positive birthing stories. Then during labour, all you'll have to do is GIVE BIRTH.

Barbara Katz Rothman highlights that "labour isn't all about just giving birth to children. A mother is also born- a strong, competent, capable mother, who trusts herself and believes in her inner power". Mary Rucklos also beautifully sums up what I've tried to express in this book so far: "the effort to separate the physical experience of childbirth from the mental, emotional, and spiritual aspects of this event has served to disempower and violate women".

When I go to sleep at night, I often see the image of childbirth before my eyes, but it's not the image of that traumatic, difficult, and painful one anymore. Now I see a woman on her knees, leaning her head softly against her man's shoulders, with strong yellow rays beaming from her. It's as if the sun, the giver of strength and power, wants to participate in this beautiful, ecstatic moment of birth to a new human. I fully believe that us women instinctively know how to give birth. It's such a shame that society takes this strength and faith away from us, trapping us in the role of 'the good patient'. Don't let them fool you. Take responsibility for yourself and for your child's birth. It's worth remembering that "whenever and however you give birth, your experience will affect your emotions, your mind, body and spirit for the rest of your life" (I.M. Gaskin). That's how cellular memory works, but you'll found out more about that in the chapter 'In the Baby's Mind'.

A space for your reflections.

AGNIESZKA PLUTA-SZKARADEK

Labour Begins in The Mind

1. Fire ring- the sensation created when the baby crowns, or in other words, presses against the crotch and stretches the tissues there (the tissues being the outer layer of the pelvic floor's muscles).

Chapter 3
In His Mind

Being a man is not at all as easy as some women may think. Some think that since the guy isn't the one to give birth, he doesn't know anything, doesn't feel, doesn't get it... I can't say I agree.

Alright, maybe you're not the one to physically give birth to this child (well, unless you're a seahorse), but there's still a lot of changes that go on in your body. It's not just your partner that's pregnant- you're in this together.

Some men notice that they experience the same symptoms that women do: nausea, breast pain (yes, guys have breasts too), stomach pains, vomiting, fatigue, and just general irritability. Some guys even grow a bit of a belly. And here the opinions of experts are divided; some think it's due to sympathetic pregnancy, others think the beer is to blame. This whole sympathetic pregnancy thing is encouraged by hormones. Their task is to help you understand what's going on during this time.

It happened! She showed you two lines on the pregnancy test. You're a dad! Yes, you already are one. Not in a month, not in six months, not when the baby is born... you're a father *now*. You became one the moment the child was conceived.

You are a wonderful father- affectionate, caring, empathetic, sensitive, and totally masculine.

Oh, I'm getting a little dreamy- but don't worry, I'm not trying to flirt! I've got my own husband of 12 years and I'm not planning on changing him anytime soon.

Whilst writing this chapter, I spent a lot of time thinking about how to write it in a way that's relatively easy to understand, but also interesting. Sara Buckley says that "the parallels between sex and childbirth are very clear, not only in terms of passion and love, but also because both these things require the same conditions- the feeling of safety and like you've got privacy", and I couldn't agree more.

At the time of conception, nobody disturbed you guys. You were alone, felt safe, and no doctor or midwife came in to take a look once every little while. Nobody took your blood pressure or stuck their fingers somewhere they should not have... so why should childbirth be any different? The exact same hormones come into play during sex as they do during childbirth, and their success depends on them being able to function correctly. Next time you're on Youtube, check out this short 8-minute film 'The Performance: sex like a birth'. You don't need to understand Italian to understand the point it's trying to make.

Scan this QR code and watch the 8-minute film on Youtube
„Push" (2021)

Labour Begins in The Mind

Task 1

How did you feel when you first found out that you're going to be a dad?

Time for your first task. Take some paper and a pen and **describe in a couple sentences your reaction, first thoughts, ideas, and feelings upon hearing the news that your family's going to get bigger.** This exercise will help you understand my next point about the teamwork needed between a man and a woman during the pregnancy, labour, and the postpartum period.

Have you done it? Great! Let's keep going.

Task 2

Imagine YOURSELF during the birth
But hey, so that it's not too easy, I'm challenging you to a

drawing contest. **Imagine YOURSELF during the birth... yes, you read that right- YOURSELF, and not your woman.** Think about where you are, what you're wearing, if you've shaved, whether it's warm or not, whether it's light or dark. Who's around you? What's the atmosphere like? Are you calm and composed, or are you nervously pacing from one corner of the room to the other?

And now think about her. Which position is she in? Where are you in that given moment? How are you reacting and behaving? Try to convey onto the paper everything that's important TO YOU during this labour. Yes, dad- YOU ARE ALSO IMPORTANT.

Thank you for that. I know that it wasn't an easy task. That task wasn't about testing your artistic abilities, but rather about trying to visualise the things that I'll be writing about over the next few pages.

You're probably reading this book for several reasons:
· Your partner made you do it
· You reached for it yourself because your mate, an experienced dad, told you that it's not all that easy
· You got it as a present and you're currently sat on your throne in the bathroom, trying to make sense of the words.

Labour Begins in The Mind

It doesn't matter what your answer is. What's important is that you're reading it. If you haven't already wondered why I'm writing to the gentlemen (i.e., to you) in such a light and humorous way, then let me quickly explain. It'll take me approximately a sentence or two... okay, maybe three.

Ever since I was a kid, I've always gotten along better with the guys rather than the girls. I chased after the ball, climbed trees, played with sticks, and basically just got on better with the opposite sex than I did with the girls, who always seemed to have some sort of problem. Whether it was the shoes that didn't match, or maybe the lipstick wasn't right, (and don't get me started on the whole 'I don't have anything to wear!'), there was always some kind of problem. As a kid, I loved my old worn-out jeans and T-shirt. My red hair and freckles that only came out in the summer didn't stop me from teasing and flirting with the boys in my own little way.

And then I met Grzesiek. He was the one that seduced *me*. Whilst I still don't enjoy getting all dressed up and doing my makeup every day, a lot of men still tell me that I've got that 'something'. I still don't really know what that 'something' is, but I have it. And that's why whilst writing this chapter, I'm thinking about *YOU*- a man whom I'll tell what childbirth really is like in a simple, playful way and explain why LABOUR BEGINS IN THE MIND.

AGNIESZKA PLUTA-SZKARADEK

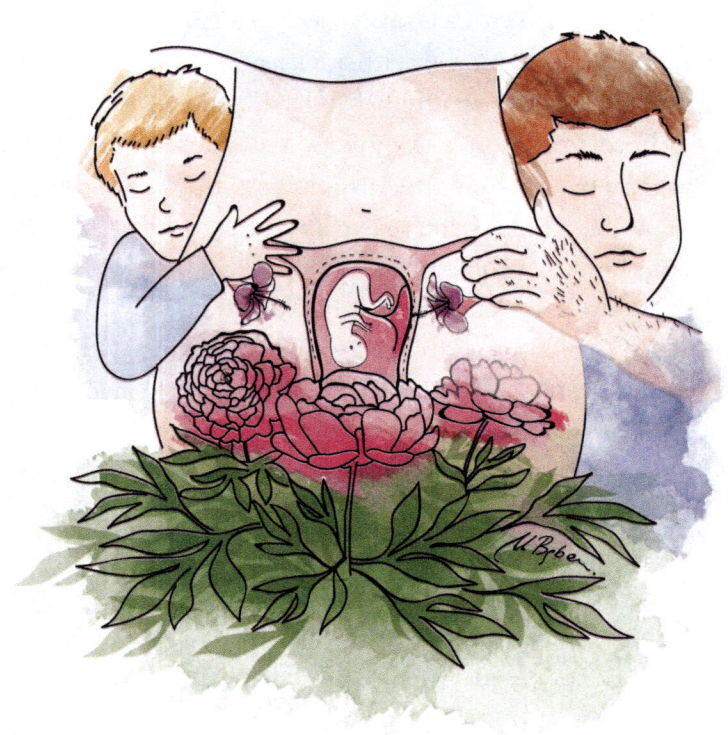

Labour Begins in The Mind

A PREGNANCY, as I'm sure you already know, lasts 280 days[1]. Some say nine months, others say ten. Doctors like to talk about the nine months of pregnancy, and scientists about the three trimesters. Either way, I would encourage you to spend this time in joy and anticipation. Remember when you were a little kid and it was the countdown to Christmas? You had an advent calendar which you would excitedly open every day and count down the days until you could finally open the presents from underneath that Christmas tree? Pregnancy is similar. You're waiting patiently because you know that at the very end...hmm. Santa Clause will come? St Nicholas? Baby Jesus? A little angel? Who used to bring the Christmas presents in your home? Ahh, it was mum that put the presents underneath the tree... it all makes sense now! Oh mums, they spend their whole lives giving us gifts.

The time will come when you will be blessed with your best present yet. Whether it's a son or a daughter, it doesn't really matter. It will be your child.

One of the first questions I ask couples during my antenatal classes which I've been giving in the UK for several years now, is a rather tricky one: "why do we use the term 'birthing school?'". Have women really forgotten that they can give birth? The answer is extremely simple- the name is completely false. It only exists for marketing purposes because the name's been long accepted by society.

We don't need to teach women how to give birth- they already know how to! Instead, let's let them discover their inner power.

For many men, the time of pregnancy is a difficult period in life. Some women give up their job in order to get the house ready- your nest- for the arrival of a very special someone. **You may now feel like there's a bigger responsibility falling on you to look after your family, as well as your family's finances and wellbeing.** It's usually men that are the main source of income in the household- ah, not that stereotype again! But when it comes to motherhood, every woman, whether she wants it or not, needs to have the time to return to their pre-pregnancy self. So, what does this entail? Throughout these nine months, **her task is to prepare herself mentally and physically for childbirth,** as well as for the care of her newborn. Michel Odent believes that "the presence of a supportive person may be more important for the mother and child than all this sophisticated new technology".

Your task is to accompany and help your woman, support her, listen to her fears and worries, share her happiness, and wipe away her joyful tears. It is your duty to be there for her when she needs you the most. Sometimes all you have to do is just be there for her. Surrender yourselves to the power of birth!

So, what can you do during those nine months? How can you prepare yourself so that you feel competent enough? I'm not telling you to attend a hundred different antenatal classes, although you're very welcome to attend mine. It's worthwhile possessing basic knowledge on the physiology of childbirth and the postpartum period. At least you'll be able to tell your friends all about your bravery and that you didn't faint! Again with the jokes-sorry. A guy fainting on the deliver suite is actually quite a rarity. But anyways, **you'll need this knowledge first and foremost to be able to defend your partner's rights, choices, and birth plan.**

Something tells me that I should probably also share with you the definition of labour contractions. To quote Ina May Gaskin, "contractions don't have to hurt". They are waves of energy which allow the woman to open up so that the baby can come out.'

Task 3

How are you going to react?

Hypothetically speaking, let's say that the labour begins at around 1am with irregular contractions. By the time morning comes, the contractions become more frequent, and they come on about every 10 minutes. You make breakfast, offer a warm bath and a massage, but the atmosphere is becoming more and more tense. So, now you're running around the house with an app which measures the contractions, trying to work out if you've packed everything for the hospital. And where are those damn car keys?! Okay, here they are. They were in your pocket. You decide to go to the hospital only when the contractions become more frequent. They're now at five minutes apart. You get into the car and off you go. You get to the hospital at around 3pm. Before they admit you, you fill out a bunch of paperwork, they ask you the same thing about a hundred times, aaaand the contractions stop... typical. But at least you managed to get your first examination of the night ...and so? Only 3cm dilated.

And now what? Please write down how you're feeling in this kind of situation and how you're acting. What you are saying to your partner as she looks deep into your eyes, searching for some sort of help, and says "how can it only be at 3cm? It's already so painful and I'm struggling to cope. What's it's gonna be like later? I won't be able to do it. Please, do something!"?

But what are you meant to do? It's not like you can give birth for her. It's us women that have been blessed by nature with the gift of bringing life into this world. **We are made for this. The ability to give birth to children has long been**

engraved in our brains. It just so happens that the world has temporarily taken this ability away from us, making us forget about it. In turn, this has made us lose faith in ourselves.

And so, you made it to the delivery suite. Suddenly, the face of a doctor with a strange smile on his face peeps out from behind a slightly ajar door. "We can pierce the amniotic sac and you will give birth faster", he suggests. And *now* it's time for you to sort yourself out! This is your time to act and react! She is already in so much pain that in a second, she will agree to just about anything, as long as it helps the pain go away. It is important that you know the consequences of piercing the amniotic sac. First of all, it limits the labour to a maximum of 24 hours. It makes the contractions significantly stronger, making them come one after another, and leaving no room for a break. Their intensity is so strong that after a while the woman will most likely ask for an epidural. If they also hook her up to an ECG, expect two more hours of her having to lie on her back, with more painful contractions and the inability to move freely. Soon after that, someone will suggest to administer synthetic oxytocin through an IV drip. Physically speaking, when the baby is in the amniotic sac, it is safe because it is surrounded by water. This water makes it easier for the baby to position itself into the birth canal. Have you ever seen a baby born in a completely preserved amniotic sac? I would highly suggest you check it out on YouTube, as it is truly something spectacular.

"Human childbirth has evolved in a way most suited to our species, so if we interfere in this perfect process, we cannot complain about the later consequences of doing so." (M. Jowitt)

AGNIESZKA PLUTA-SZKARADEK

I am important

Labour Begins in The Mind

YOU DID IT. You protected her birth plan. Ina May Gaskin, who's often referred to as a 'hippie midwife', claims that "if a woman doesn't look like a Goddess when giving birth, it means that someone isn't treating her like one". And she's absolutely right. A woman in labour is like water and fire, earth and air, the sun and the moon, a violent storm and calm waves both at the same time- you'll be able to see each one of these elements reflected in her face. Because during birth, not only a baby is born, but also a mother (I. Dembińska). Your job is to support your woman as she walks the road to a beautiful transformation.

The hours go by like in an action film. The labour sticks to its own rhythm and goes on at its own pace. The contractions are getting stronger. You feel a little disoriented but rest assured, you know what you're doing. You're both in a new, smelly situation. Well unless if you happen to like the hospital smell... I know I don't. Just thinking about it makes my skin crawl. So then along comes the midwife, checks the dilation, and in a beaming voice she announces "10cm. Let's do it!".

A flood of emotions overcome you: joy, excitement, thrill, a little fear. **It's a feeling similar to the one when you're reaching the peak of the biggest, fastest, highest and just all-around the best rollercoaster ever built. You get to the top and you know there's no way back now- you've got to go through with it. Only except that this ride has an amazing ending (purpose)- you getting to hold *your* baby.** The baby that you have created will truly appear in your strong, manly arms.

Yes, it's at this point that tears are very welcome and no, they are not a sign of weakness. You are a strong man. A man of many women's dreams. But remember, to your woman you are the one and only, special, exceptional, and most handsome man. Even though not a mere second ago she was screaming that she'll kill you, that it's all your fault that it hurts, that she's never giving birth again, that you have a lifetime ban for sex… yeah, everything that you just heard her shout during labour, let it slide. I understand that these words are hurtful ones, but truly, coming from a woman, just forgive her. **During labour she transforms into an animal protecting her territory. She enters her intimate world of giving birth and is unable to rationally control the situation.** And if she tries to control it, your job is to do everything you can to make her cerebral cortex stop working for just a little while (well okay, maybe a little longer than that).

During labour, a woman's thinking is dominated by the so-called primal brain, that is, the part of the brain that's responsible for all our primal instincts. If the woman does not feel safe, cared for, and loved, she won't let the reptile brain take over and will keep trying to take control of the situation. But this will just make childbirth longer, harder, more difficult, more physically exhausting, and even much more painful for her. And that's something neither of us want for her.

Both my goal as well as probably yours too, is for this birth to be as smooth as possible. When I say that though, I don't mean pain-free, because the pain means that the birth is taking its proper course. Pain is the result of contractions, and without them, it's impossible to give birth to a baby.

Therefore, both my goal and your goal during labour should be to support the woman in such a way so that she achieves longer and stronger contractions, accepting them as life's gift.

Understanding the role of contractions will help you get over the idea of wanting to do anything and everything to make sure your beloved woman does not 'suffer'. **I totally get that, but please, support and care for your woman, let her experience the birth in her own way, but for the love of God, don't tell her that you can see how much she's suffering… SHE'S NOT SUFFERING! SHE'S GIVING BIRTH!!**

Jokes like "the pain a woman experiences during labour is so strong that a man may only be able to experience it when he gets a fever" don't make me laugh at all. Jokes that talk about how no one has ever met a guy who, after a kick in the balls, says "I'd like to do it again someday" are simply pathetic to say the least, but then it's not like women giving birth several times is a novelty. All in all, it shows that childbirth can be a beautiful, profound experience that does not have to be associated with trauma, pain, and suffering.

I would also just like to turn your attention to the fact that **we can sperate pain into two different types: the physical and the emotional one.**

Our job (yours as a partner and mine as a doula), is to be there for the woman as she gives birth, and to support her in such a way so that after birth, she doesn't have to go through emotional pain.

"A naturally behaving woman follows her body's wisdom, which guides her through childbirth so that she doesn't solely have to rely on those around her but can also trust herself. **Trust is the best investment you can make when it comes to childbirth.** When we believe that a woman's body knows how to give birth (...), we rely on all the births which have been occurring for millions of years" (K. Oleś). This is a very difficult and responsible task, but I believe that you can rise to the challenge. If you ever feel like you need some advice about it, don't be shy, just send me a message. (kontakt@polskaszkolarodzenia.co.uk).

After an indescribable moment, you hear a sound that not only reaches your ears, but also your heart. **This is the moment when you fall in love for the second time (or maybe it's your third or a hundredth time). You look at this small, helpless, shivering little creature which rests upon the chest of a woman- the mother of your child- and you feel your eyes flood with tears of joys.** Don't be shy, let it out. Love, cuddle, kiss, be, experience. This is your time.

I'm sure you've probably already heard about the possibility of giving birth at home. **Personally, I believe that men can be involved most in a homebirth, rather than any other type of birth**. I don't remember where I heard or read those words first, but as soon as I find the source, I will post it on my Facebook page, which I would now sincerely invite you to check out.

It would seem as though you wouldn't need to know a lot about breastfeeding- after all, it's not you who has to take care of it. In practice, it often occurs that if you don't know an appropriate amount about breastfeeding or you're not personally convinced about the benefits of natural breastfeeding, you'll quickly reach for the bottle. We're living in a very fast-paced world nowadays when people don't want to fight or care for the more difficult things. **I must warn you now that breastfeeding is harder than both the pregnancy and birth put together.** It probably won't be a surprise when I share Magda Karpienia's words with you and tell you that "the further away from civilisation, the more common natural feeding is, and the fewer problems arise from it". Because we live in a fast-paced world, where huge gleaming billboards gush not breast milk but bottle milk, it's easier to give in and conclude that no one's ever died from baby formula milk. And no, they haven't, but it really is possible to do things differently. So, want to learn a thing or two about breastfeeding?

Great. Let's start with the fact that the size, nipple, or breast size does not matter. It's a bit like with a penis... size really doesn't matter. "The tool is only as effective as the skillfulness of the hands that wield it"- and that's exactly what breastfeeding's like.

Women's breastmilk is made from blood, or specifically plasma, a component of blood. The main hormones responsible for lactation are prolactin and oxytocin. **Did you know that even women who have not given birth to a child but have adopted and blessed it with love and care, can also breastfeed?** There is only one reason why they wouldn't be able to- if they didn't actually have breasts (for example, due to an amputation after cancer).

Now ask yourself one thing: do cows drink human milk? No. Do puppies drink cat's milk? Also no. Then why do people give their children modified powdered milk? (Modified- even the very name sounds terrible. Don't you think? MO-DI-FIED, or in other words, 'changed' in some way.)

Breastmilk is perfect for the baby at every stage of their development. Even if the baby arrives earlier than planned, such food is the ideal nourishment for it, and in addition, it strengthens the baby's immunity. Milk production begins as early as in the 16th week of pregnancy, so it may happen that during certain evening 'activities' with your wife, a few drops may come out of her breast. This happens from oxytocin and arousal... hm, I'm sure you already know how to make that happen. Breast milk is usually sweet in taste, so you have two options: swallow and not say anything or spit it out and say something. Either way, the choice is yours, but so are the consequences of your woman's reaction.

THE MOTHER'S milk is more than just food for the baby. To have a happy baby, what you really need to provide it with is closeness, the warmth of their mother's body and milk. The baby gets all of this when being breastfed. By sucking on the breast, the baby stimulates it and promotes milk production. So, the more often we breastfeed, the better the lactation is. **Breastfeeding provides food, drink (hydration), calms and soothes, allows the baby to feel safe, lets the baby be close to their mother's heartbeat and be surrounded by her scent, puts the baby to sleep, and lets it rest in the nurturing arms of their mother.**

> *"Breastfeeding is a tool which nature has blessed women with so that with one action she can satisfy all the needs of a little human-being"* (M. Karpienia).

As Magda Karpienia points out, successful breastfeeding requires three conditions: knowledge, support, and faith.

When we talk **knowledge**, we're referring specifically to the physiology behind the way the food gets made. Oh, and by the way, **there's no such thing as a special diet that you have to be on when breastfeeding, so you can cook her anything she likes as long as it's healthy**. Food, as I just mentioned, is made from the blood. So unfortunately, that fish and chips has no chance of reaching the boobs...there's just no possible way. However, since we're on the topic, it's also worth noting that some allergens can enter the bloodstream. But this is something you'll only need to worry about if you child starts developing symptoms of a food allergy.

It is especially important that she receives a lot of **support** from you and other people closest to her. Here, we're talking specifically about emotional support. If breastfeeding is painful, then this means that something needs to be adjusted. Emotional support also means searching for solutions if there is such a need. It's best to go see a lactation consultant. During this meeting, (which ideally takes place in your home- I travel to see my clients because I cannot imagine making a mother with a newborn queue in some clinic), the lactation consultant will check the breastfeeding technique. If the consultant decides that there are no issues with the technique, then the next step will be to check the baby's reflexes and if the baby has tongue-tie. I must also mention that it's very often during these consultations that I'll see a crying baby and a very tired and sore mother who just puts the nipple into the baby's mouth in the hopes that it'll stop crying. That's not exactly what this is about.

Breastfeeding is not something you can practice during the pregnancy and that's what makes it so hard. The mother and the baby both have to learn each other's ways, and this takes some time.

The breast must be given to the baby, and not forced into their mouth. The baby should grasp the entire areola of the nipple as deeply and firmly as it can. And trust me, no, the baby will not choke.

And finally, **belief**; belief in the fact that breasts are made for feeding and are not only just a purpose for sexual pleasure. The belief that you as a father chooses what's best for the child- you're giving your child a mother to have at their entire disposal (just for a little while, don't panic). Belief in the fact that when you both finally learn how to breastfeed, you will have a very satisfied and happy woman at home.

And now let's talk about the financial side of things. **Grab a calculator and go calculate just how much money you can save by feeing your baby naturally.** I'll help you out:

In the first 24 hours after birth, a baby needs 5-7ml of milk per feeding. On the second day, about 15ml, and after a week, 30ml. The smallest portion you can make from baby formula is 30ml...so you'll either be overfeeding your baby or throwing your milk away. And now let's calculate...

With an average of ten feeds a day, a box of baby formula usually lasts about a week. The older the baby gets, the less it lasts- about two or three days. The cost of one box of baby formula costs approximately about £10. By the time the baby is six months old, 26 weeks would have passed. This is the minimum amount of time during which the baby feeds only from milk, without being given anything else to eat or drink.

26 weeks x 3 boxes = 78 boxes

78 boxes of baby formula x £10 = £780

And on top of all that, you have to also include the cost of buying bottles, teats, a bottle steriliser, and also a bottle warmer... **so all together that comes to about £1000!** And so, what's it gonna be? Bottle or breastfeeding?

When writing this book, I wanted to firstly address the ladies, because when it comes to childbirth, it's us who have the most important job. Understanding childbirth and preparing for it takes a lot of time. I don't know whether you've read the first chapter or not, but I would encourage you to do so. You'll see how long it took even me to understand this simple, yet so difficult life process that is the birth of a child.

"The most important thing is that the child is born healthy" ... pardon my French but that's a load of bullshit. The most important thing in childbirth is that a healthy, strong, and proud mother is born. The birth of a healthy baby is a subservient to this.

And I'm not even exaggerating. Do you know why I chose to write about this here? Maybe you're even wondering why I'm addressing you in the first place. You have to know that I also care about you, a man who has come to be faced with quite a challenge. You've got a sweet little creature sleeping in your arms whilst you partner rests in the bedroom. Your partner: a strong woman who has just given birth to your child. In literature they describe her current state as 'puerperium'. Experts consider it to be the fourth trimester of a pregnancy. And this makes sense because during the postpartum period, her body and hormones return to their initial state, i.e., the time before pregnancy. **This process lasts six weeks and it's up to you, my dear, to decide how it's going to go. You are now in command of this ship. Go put on your captain's hat and grab the helm.**

The postpartum period requires an enormous amount of patience, understanding, as well as mental and physical support. It's a time when the woman becomes flooded with emotions she doesn't necessarily have much control over. However, you have control over what's happening around you. You are now not only responsible for yourself, but also for her and the child.

How you act, how you speak, and what you do greatly influences how she will react. And it's going to be this way now for the rest of your lives.

It is easy to just keep writing and writing about the postpartum period, but I will try to keep it short and sweet when telling you the most important things you should make sure to take care of.

The first of these things is food. They say that the way to the man's heart is through his stomach, but in this situation, it's the other way around. The physical exertion which childbirth undoubtedly is makes it crucial to replenish the lost energy reserves. So, tonight it's the ship's Captain that's taking over the kitchen. What's for dinner, Chef? Also remember to make sure that your loved one drinks plenty of water. When you're caring for a baby, it's easy to forget about your own needs or postpone them and say, "I'll do it later". Hence why you'll always hear mum's saying, "I'll go pee in a sec", "I'll have some water later", "I'll eat something when the baby falls asleep" but the hours just go by. You forget about your full bladder, the stomach gets used to less food, and the body starts to dehydrate. The woman then begins to feel tired, first physically, and then emotionally. Why not make her breakfast in bed while she breastfeeds? She feeds the baby and you feed her. It's physical, practical, and direct. Go on, I know you can do it.

Now that you've taken care of your treasure, it's time to take care of the rest of your ship. Your ship is drowning in dirty laundry, the dishes in the sink are overflowing, the floor is sticky, and I'm pretty sure there's something moving in the cat's litter box. It just so happens that all your sailors are on holiday and so the Captain has to also become the deckhand and clean up.

Such help during the postpartum period is enough and allows the woman to recover quicker. Some recover faster, others slower. **Make sure to give the mother of your child as much time as she needs.**

As you already know, during the first few weeks of life, the baby is closely attached to their mother, but this absolutely does NOT mean that you have been forgotten about or demoted to the role of the cook and cleaner. You are important! You're the Head of the family, who quietly watches and waits to spring into action. A one-month-old baby would certainly love to cuddle up to your warm body. **Learning to care for such a small and delicate creature takes time and patience. Give yourself time too.** You don't have to know right away how to change a nappy, especially if the umbilical cord stump is still in the way. Practising this on a doll during antenatal classes is not the same thing as when you're trying to change the nappy of a fussing and crying baby. But rest assured, you can do it, Dad!

I want to tell you that **it's possible to understand childbirth and to plan everything perfectly in your head.** I want to tell you that labour starts in the mind, *your* mind. I want to thank you for enduring these last few pages with me, which I hope to have at least helped you a little bit in preparing for and getting to grips with what's to come.

To me, the greatest treasure is childbirth and natural breastfeeding. Emilia Lichtenberg-Kokoszka notes that "the best and most beautiful births are when nature is not disturbed". Therefore, before the baby comes, you both should be reading and thinking lots, so that during labour you can give yourselves over to the power of birth. It is something that nature has created us for. It was given to us for free, yet we do not want to take advantage of it these days. We prefer to pay for everything. We pay for a private doctor, a midwife, a hospital, for baby formula and bottles. We also pay a high emotional price for something that's happened because at some point we made a bad decision. I don't want to write that it's always the same everywhere because that's simply not true. In my opinion, the vast majority of births are unnecessarily medicalised. It is a huge pharmaceutical money machine, but I will not dwell on that here.

Maybe it'd be worth thinking about how and where your child will be born? Maybe in your house?

Task 4

How and where will your child be born?

A space for your reflections.

Labour Begins in The Mind

1. Other sources say that pregnancy lasts 266 days. The difference is due to the fact that some count it from the first day of the last period, while some count it from ovulation-the time when fertilisation occurred.

Chapter 4
In the Baby's Mind

"These are my first hours. I'm the youngest in the family. I can feel you, Mum! I am so little, but I can hear you. I'm snuggling into your belly and the rhythm of your beating heart is soothing to me. It's late autumn and it gets dark outside quickly. I like it when you rest, Mum. The soft touch of your favourite blanket and a cup of warm tea in your hands makes your heart beat slower, it's calmer. This makes me feel calmer, too. I can hear how happy Daddy is. Have you told him that I'm a girl yet? How do you know that anyway? Nobody's told you that yet. Ahh, Mummy, you're the best!

Mummy, it feels so good to be living under your heart. It makes me feel safe. I'm just as happy as you are that only it's 40 more weeks and we'll finally be able to see each other. Hey, did you know that I'm already 3mm big? My heart beats steadily... can you hear it? The midwife will use this thing, it's called a foetal heart monitor[1], and you'll be able to hear me.

Today marks another week of us living together! I'm so sorry that you sometimes feel sick in the morning. I really don't want to cause you any problems. It's the hormones, I'm sure of it. I am a girl after all. Girls always blames their hormones. It's actually a pretty good excuse. When I'll be coming out, I'll also say that it's the hormones that picked that specific date!

Mum, I can hear you singing carols. What's happening around you? Why is Daddy getting angry that Christmas is coming but that the house is a mess? Is it because of me, Mummy, that you don't have any energy? I want this Christmas which I keep hearing you and Daddy talking about to be filled with happiness, warmth, and love. I don't actually know what 'Christmas' even means, but I have this feeling that it's this nice time which we can spend with those closest to us. You and I are also so close, Mummy!

Sometimes in the evenings, when you go to bed, I can hear you breathing. Your heartbeat is like a lullaby to me. I often think about what it will be like when we get to see each other on the other side of the belly. Will you cuddle me? Will it be as cosy and warm as it is here?

Oh, Mummy, Happy New Year! I know you can't feel it yet, but I'm jumping up and down from excitement. I'm an energetic little one, just like you. I really want to meet you and to touch your hair.

Mummy, Mummy, wake up! Today we're going to our first scan- I'm already 12 weeks old! You'll finally be able to see me. I am so happy. Even though I'm still so small, it would be awesome if you could see all of me. I'm smiling at you and Daddy; I can feel that he's there too.

You know, sometimes when I'm playing with the umbilical cord, I imagine us playing with a skipping rope. Maybe that sounds a little funny, because I don't even really know what a skipping rope is, but I can imagine us doing it together.

Are we always going to be doing things together? Will you always be close to me? I like listening to your heartbeat and feeling the warmth of your body.

Ahh, yes! I think you've finally felt me move! I heard you call Daddy over so that he could put his hand on your belly and feel me move. I'm moving round and round so you can both feel me. I am so happy that we'll finally be able to see each other soon.

Mum, do you remember... hmm, of course you remember! **I can feel everything that's happening around you right now. I can feel all your emotions, as well as Daddy's and even Granny's.** And even though I don't know how this is possible, my body will be able to remember this forever and ever. Please, make sure my birth is a beautiful one. I want you to feel special because you are- the one and only. You're MY MUM after all.

Mummy, I'm getting bigger and bigger, and I can feel my little home getting tighter. I'm a little scared because I'm not sure what's going to happen to me, but I trust that I will be safe because you'll be with me the whole time.

For a few weeks now, something has been squeezing me slightly. I've even gotten used to it and like the cuddles, but I've been feeling it more and more since yesterday. I'm pretty sure this is the moment I've heard you talk so much about.

Don't be afraid, it's my job to be born. I know how to do it. Just let me do it at my own pace. Please don't rush me. We both want my birth to be a safe one. Let me be born the way we both need me to be born. We're ready for this. I'll be letting you know that everything is okay, Mummy. You don't need to worry about me. My little heart will beat for you.

Something incredible happened in my tiny little head and a certain hormone let the whole body know- both mine and yours- that it was time. Your uterus has started working in such a way that I could properly position myself for my way out. I'm using my little legs to push myself out because I'm feeling cramped, but it's okay, we can do this. We have time.[2]

You know, it's been a while since I've heard some good music. Maybe you'll dance with Daddy? Sway your hips a bit, I like it when you do that. Get ready because soon we'll be dancing together all night long. **I'll be in your arms, and you'll be in Daddy's**. Oh, it will be so wonderful! I know that you're also very excited but that every time another contraction comes, you doubt whether you can really do it. Mummy dearest, I won't let you get hurt! I will come out in a way that will be comfortable for both of us. **I don't want you having to experience pain stronger than you can handle.** We've been connected for so long that I know how much I can give you and how much you'll take.

Thank you for preparing for my birth, Mum. Thank you so much for letting me be born the way that I want to be born. This is one of the most important first tasks in my life... thank you for believing in me.

This will allow me to believe in myself when I'm older. I've got my whole life ahead of me, and I don't know what it'll be like yet, but I do know that the way I'm born will have a significant impact on the way I react to stress, failure, and problems at school.

Mum, thank you so much for letting me live so close to your heart, and for giving me a safe and cosy home. Thank you for working so hard to avoid those people that say that women suffer when giving birth. You will not suffer; you'll just give birth. **Only the women who are afraid suffer. Their feelings of pain are much greater and stronger because they're not open to welcoming new life.** "What makes birth so full of terror is not so much the pain as the fear." (F. Laboyer). But you, Mummy dearest, you're not fearful. You feel strong, you're sure of yourself, you're surrounded by love and respect, full of grace and your inner feminine power.

AGNIESZKA PLUTA-SZKARADEK

I am calm and relaxed

Labour Begins in The Mind

When I'll be coming out, please, make sure it's silent. Actually no, not you. **Let Daddy take care of the silence, the dimmed lights in the room and us being surrounded with warmth.** Don't let me be blinded by the harsh brightness of the lamps, and don't let my ears be flooded with loud noises either. Up until this moment, surrounded by the sound of gentle waters, I've lived peacefully. I've heard the beating of your heart, the movement of your bowels, and the sound of Daddy's muffled voice. All these outside sounds will be new, loud, and sharp to me. Even though my senses have been working for a long time now, I'm still very delicate and sensitive.

Just a few more contractions and I'll be with you. I want to feel safe. So lay me on your tummy, wrap your warm hands around me, and let me savour your smell. Give me some time, just a little more time- please don't cut me off from you just yet, I'm still using the umbilical cord to breathe. My lungs are ready, but I don't want my first ever gasp of air to be painful. They are still filled with amniotic fluids, and I don't want to remember my first breath feeling like drowning. I'm about to spit the waters out, just give me a second. I'll be fine. In the meantime, speak to me in my language- the universal language, for which no words are needed; a language understood by the whole world. **YOU are my whole world. Speak to me in the language of LOVE.**

Talk to me in the way that lovers talk and look at each other. They don't need words. They just sit gazing at each other, touching each other, caressing each other with slightly sweaty hands, gently brushing their lips against each other's bodies, enjoying every breath. I don't need light to see and feel you.

Mum, Dad, fall in love with me. Together, let us cherish this moment of my birth. It would be the most beautiful gift I could ever receive from you.

I don't need toys, decorations for my room or even clothes. My skin is covered in vernix which is there to protect me. Please, don't wipe it off, don't bathe me, don't dress me just yet. Let me enjoy your warmth. I can already smell that familiar scent. I'm following the smell of the colostrum and I know what I have to do. Don't worry, I can handle it. I am strong. I used my little legs to push myself out of your belly to be born, and now I'm using them to push myself away from your belly to survive. Teach me to be independent but safe at the same time. I'm not jumping into the abyss; I know that you're here and that you're protecting me. Now I will crawl my way over to your breasts all alone, for there my award awaits me: your golden food.

"Childbirth should be your greatest achievement, not your greatest fear." (J. Weideman)

Thanks to you believing in yourself and in me, my birth has not been marked by an emotional scar. Such scars remain painful our whole lives. Children born with fear will struggle to cope with irrational fears their whole life. They will be insecure, confused, and fearful children. But not me. I had the most beautiful birth in the world...in this little world of mine."

The wonderful mental coach Olga Barbara Pietrzak will tell us a little more about emotional wounds and cellular memory. Thanks to this woman, a mama bear showed me the path to motherhood and allowed fear and hurt to leave my body[3]. I invited her to share her knowledge in this book because I myself have witnessed how she helps women find their bearings on the path to motherhood, as well as how she supports them and liberates them from fear.

The next section of this book contains many interesting facts about perinatal psychology. What you are about to read may give you lots to think about and may also seem a little disheartening and bleak. Compare this description of childbirth with the previous one and think about what the next generation could be like. Maybe if we just come together, we could change the way our children are born.

Olga Barbara Pietrzak, co-author of this chapter

Thank you, Agnieszka, for allowing me to write a chapter for your book! Thank you for trusting me. I will do my best to pass on my knowledge to your mentees and clients in the simplest way possible. And thank you to you, too, for reading this book and this section of it and for all your interest.

My name is Olga B. Pietrzak - I am a life coach and therapist for addiction and codependency. I am constantly learning, drawing on the diversity that the world and science have to offer, so that I can help all my clients as effectively as possible. Before I got into mental and emotional support, I took a long road which had many twists and turns. Firstly, I needed to find myself and establish a deep relationship with myself. Following on from the title of this book, I notice that also the relationship with oneself starts in the mind. More specifically, it starts the moment you correctly understand one's history, thought patterns and emotions. This can all be either positive or negative. You can have positive beliefs about yourself and the world around you, or negative ones. Instead of flourishing and trusting yourself and the world, these negative beliefs cause you to treat life as a problem. Not only this, but instead of gaining life's energy, you neglect it. As a result, you lose this energy and have no strength for almost anything. Sound familiar?

In order to understand yourself at these deepest levels, it's worth starting to get to know yourself from the very beginning of your existence. But that's from when? From birth? From the moment you were conceived? Or maybe even earlier? **Total Biology (more specifically, Recall Healing) tells us that the emotional state of the parents is already relevant to our life around nine months before conception.** Specifically, it refers to the 'family tree: generational syndrome'. Gilbert Renaud describes it in this way: "we define the project/purpose **as a goal unconsciously adopted by the child, who then throughout their life strives towards its realisation.** The goal stems from events and emotions that were experienced by the parents (or just one of them) shortly before the child's conception, during pregnancy, during the child's birth and/or during the first year of life".

We've known for a long time now that the prenatal period for the baby is very important. It takes a quick Google search to find many articles and scientific studies which tell us that **the baby in the womb feels the same as the mother.** This knowledge is already quite widespread. Why is it then that so many women seem to know and hear this information, but do not prepare themselves mentally and emotionally for pregnancy? Birthing schools are becoming more and more popular, and classes are available both in-person and online, and yet such a small percentage of couples take advantage of them. Agnieszka! I am so thankful and glad to have met you. Thanks to you I know so much, but at the same time, still so little about homebirths and the role of a doula.

Wait a minute... Exactly, when should we start getting in touch with the midwife? Or the doula? What about the gynaecologist? We usually do it when we're preparing for the birth of the baby. But what does this preparation consist of exactly? **Perhaps it would be much easier and even better for us if we started these preparations before we even got pregnant** rather than, as it has become so widely accepted, during the pregnancy. **We could, for example, choose to undergo our own therapy, so that our child does not have to 'inherit' painful memories or negative beliefs.** The child would be able to grow up in a warm family atmosphere, free of recurring thoughts that burden us, and not in a home in which the parents' relationship is so-so and there's hope in the child to save the relationship. I would highly encourage conscious family planning. When I say that, I do not mean using contraception, but **taking full responsibility for the new human being created from you, Woman and Man.** It will be very important to this child how they came into being, how they developed, how they were born and what their first stage of life was like in this world.

Some of us were planned, others not so much. This detail is pretty significant, but equally important is how the parents received the news that their family is about to get bigger. Regardless of these circumstances, the MIRACLE is that this one particular sperm made it to this one particular egg cell at just the right time... Because that is how your journey began. Your lifelong journey of a MIRACLE CHILD. Yes, I'm talking about YOU. Because YOU still are this miracle, even though you may sometimes forget about it or not remember it at all. Whether you like it or not, this small, vulnerable miracle child still lives inside you.

What came first, the body and then the soul? Or maybe it was the soul first and then the body? There's lots of different theories and ideas about this. But if you are here, right now, in this world, then it means that you have both a body and a soul. And if we add the mind into this mix then there, we have it- a miracle.

Body

Mind

Soul

You're probably now asking yourself, **"how do I trust my body?"**. Well, when talking about the miracle of conception, it took a sexual act for the physical cells to have a chance to meet. And then the sperm and the egg cell knew exactly what they had to do. After all, they come from your body and your partner's body. They're your body, or more precisely, a cell of your body. They know their purpose and what their objective is. Then, once the objective's been achieved, that is, once the egg cell and the sperm cell have successfully met, the fertilised egg cell also knows what it's supposed to do next. It knows perfectly well that cell division is to occur. Then it is to nest in the uterus and build up the new body step by step. And as a result, around the 40th week, the baby is ready to leave the womb to begin their adventure on planet Earth. So, are you still doubting whether you can trust your body and whether it knows what it's doing?

You see… you don't have to do anything (except in exceptional circumstances), and you don't have to interfere in any way so that the child, from the moment of the egg cell's fertilisation, can develop properly until birth. And in fact, if we have the right approach to our own body, we won't have to interfere with it in any way for the rest of our lives. That egg cell and that sperm cell know exactly that from fertilisation a child is to be created, that child being the future YOU, your child and everyone else. This is not something you have to know or remember to do. You don't have to press any buttons so that the nervous system, heart, eyes, or kidneys get created at the right time, or that the formation of bones or a liver or anything else is right on time either. It's just not your job to do. **Before you see those two lines on the pregnancy test, your baby's heart will already be beating because it starts its work on the 21st day after conception.** You simply trust, because you know that your body and your partner's body know what they're doing because they have the ability and the knowledge to do so. Your baby's body too, just like yours, has the wisdom to take care of itself, to create and regenerate itself. You simply trust and wait for everything to happen when it's meant to happen. Do you still really have any doubts that the body knows what it's doing?

It can therefore be concluded that the cells of our body, like for example the egg cell and the sperm cell, have the knowledge which helps them carry out their plan. Let's not prevent them from doing so, but let's trust them instead! **It is said that the body remembers everything and that there's something called cellular memory**. According to the book 'The Biology of Belief' by Bruce Lipton, DNA and genes are controlled by outside stimuli. Therefore**, we can influence the state of our body through the way we think – this can be through either negative or positive thoughts.** We often have a negative influence on ourselves, even though our body and our child's body know perfectly well what they have to do. For example, childbirth takes too long because we have certain negative beliefs about it which we have not yet worked through. But it doesn't have to be this way! You could give birth at a regular pace, without panic and fear, filled with trust, excitement, and love, all whilst feeling safe. So, positive and negative impact... how does it relate to conception and the prenatal period?

AGNIESZKA PLUTA-SZKARADEK

I have got power to bring new life in to the world

So, here we go.
Here's a little sneak peek into a diary:

The time before conception

"You are both still troubled by a burning sense of guilt within you. A shame that prevents you from moving on to the next stage of your spiritual growth. Both you and your family are burdened by the secret abortion you had a few years ago. You won't do it again. No way. This memory burns like fire. You don't want to have any more children, and if you do, abortion won't even be an option. You know the emotional pain that it causes and that **this pain gets engraved in the body and memory for life.** That is why I will come to you, as we have agreed, so that you can understand that there's more out there than just the guilt, and so that I myself can take this toxic guilt and toxic shame away from you. Yes, I can see it now. The moment has come. My soul is about to descend to Earth because it's happened, femininity and masculinity have met so that I can begin my life... I see you, Mum. I see you, Dad. I choose you to be my parents because I want to be your child[4]. We agreed on this a long time ago. You need me so that I can teach you something and I need you to be able to do the same. This is what we agreed on many years ago with God and the Angels.

FIRST TRIMESTER

I exist. I am simply a human being made up of cells that keep dividing. They divide and divide and divide... and what happens next? I don't know. But for now, I am dividing.

Mum, I am in you. I have nested. I feel you. I am made from

Mum and Dad. You made love, that's why I am in you. That day you had a good day. You were on holiday, you sang, you danced, and you had a fun time. You got carried away with the fun and alcohol. You let yourselves relax. Mum, you had a feeling you might get pregnant. You didn't really want to, but Dad insisted.

I am programmed to make decisions on having children under the influence of alcohol. Yes, this is my program. I have it after you. I am also programmed to allow men to cross my boundaries.

I have a heart. My heart is beating. Boom, boom, boom. I'm in you, Mum. I'm here. I feel everything My nervous system remembers everything. You're afraid you might be pregnant. I'm another child of yours now. An unplanned one. You're afraid because you have a feeling that that day was a fertile day. **I feel you because I am you. Are you scared of me, Mum?**

I'm a little girl. My eyes, ears, hands and legs are forming. And you probably already know that you're pregnant. **Are you scared? Are you afraid of me? Is the world that scary? I don't want to feel scared, but I do because I am you.**

I already have so many internal organs. I'm growing so well. It's just happening on its own. But without you, Mum, and without you, Dad, this wouldn't have been possible. If it wasn't for your love, then I wouldn't have been able to grow. Support me and my little body will know what to do.

Mum, I'm a girl! I knew I would be. Isn't this so great? Oh, you wanted a boy... are you ashamed of me? But why are you ashamed of me? You already have some clothes for me after my older brother? Are clothes more important than my gender?

I have eyes. I can't open them yet, but I can't wait to see you. My heart is beating harder and harder. It's full. I'm alive, I'm truly alive! I AM ALIVE. I love you, Mum. I am you.

Mum, are you worried? **Do you not want me? What's the matter? I don't feel safe. Why are you crying? Is it because of me? Is it because Dad doesn't want me? I'm scared, Mum.** I feel very strange. Do you want to 'get rid of' me? I'm scared of those words. Why do you want to 'get rid of' me? You're saying something about money. Dad is also scared. When you guys are scared, so am I. You're the only ones I can trust, the only ones I can rely on. After all, I am made from you. I'm made from your cells, your emotions, your decisions, and the consequences of those decisions. Why are you talking about me and money? I'm too tiny for that. After all, I'm growing on my own and at my own pace. I don't need money for that. Why am I associating money with fear?

SECOND TRIMESTER

Mum! I already have full arms and legs. I can move them. Wow, this is so much fun! I'm bouncing around. Can you feel me doing it? Can you?? Tell me that you can feel me. Tell me anything. Tell me how great it is that I'm with you. Tell me that it's so great that you can finally feel me. No? You can't feel me? **You don't want to feel me? But why not? Okay mum, I'll be quiet. I'll be quietly existing inside of you. I won't disturb you. You don't want me, but I can't survive without you. Love me... I just need you to love me.**

Mum, are you happy that you can feel me? Oh mum, thank you for being happy! Can I stop being afraid now? I'm afraid you'll want to 'get rid of' me again. But no... not this time! I can feel your love. You told me that you love me! Do you really love me? Yes, you do. I can feel it. **I can feel more of your emotions than you may think. I feel everything.**

Are you scared of Dad? Dad doesn't love me, right? Dad didn't want me... he only wanted sex... he didn't want *me*. But I can feel that you're protecting me, that you love me to the moon and back. You're so happy now. I'm smiling at you because I can feel that you're happy. Your body is happy and mine feels more and more safe because I can feel the peace in you. You are peaceful and so I am peaceful too. I am YOU.

You're arguing with Dad. I can hear it. What are you arguing about? You're arguing about... no, I don't understand it. Oh, you're arguing about money again. You have doubts. Is the money really that important? I guess it is since that's what you're arguing about. It's apparently more important than me. **You talk more about money than you do about me. Money is more important than me. So now I know that money will be important in my own life, too**. **More important than me.** Yes, I know now that money is important. I know it all because that's what you guys are feeling and Mum, I am YOU. It's a symbiosis.

Mum, I'm breathing! I am breathing! I am breathing for you! We'll see each other soon. I'm already so big and yet not too long ago, I was just a little seed! I already have a lot in my little body, but I still need to be inside of you. Without you I don't exist, without you I can't survive. I'm such a lovely little girl. Are you happy to be having a girl? Or would you maybe prefer a boy? Are others telling you that it's better to have a boy? But I can feel that you want me just the way I am. I feel safe inside of you. I know that you accept me, but what's all this talk about money?

Dad, did you feel it?? You did! You felt me! And you're happy about it! You feel emotional! You call me your little girl. Dad, please don't 'get rid of' me. I love you. I am you and Mum. I love you guys. It's thanks to you, after all, that I'm even here in this world. I don't want to be a burden. I want to be your little-big joy. I love you guys. Talk to me as much as possible. It feels so good when I can feel your love, joy, emotion. These emotions are so nice. They build me up; it's so wonderful.

It's so tight! I'm cramped! There's not much room here but I can feel you touching me. Your touch is so nice. I like it when you touch me too, Dad. Touch me. Be close to me. This touch feels so safe. I need this kind of safety.

Ooo, I can hear my siblings talking to me! Why didn't they talk to me earlier? Were they also afraid? Did they also not want me? They didn't know about me. But why didn't they know about me? Why am I only hearing them for the first time now?

I was a secret. An unplanned baby. You were ashamed of me... that's why in the back of your heads you had thoughts about getting rid of me. I'm going to have a little cry to myself now... **I don't want to be your problem. I don't want you to have a problem with me.** I want you guys to be happy. I love it when you're happy. I love the affection, gratitude, and when you feel love and euphoria.

THIRD TRIMESTER

It's so bright! Mum, is it summer? So bright! I can't sleep. But you're feeling good. You're stroking your belly, lying in the long green grass. It's blissful to you. I am also blissful, but just turn off that light. I can't sleep! But it feels good to be with you. This is bliss. Why are you thinking about money again? I get it, it's important. It's already coded in me.

Mum, I can hear you now! I can feel you I know what you're eating. Oh, this chocolate is so good. And those pickles. But the peppers not so much.

Mum, why are you eating so much? Are you stress eating? Do we have to eat when we're stressed? Does eating help you survive?

I feel so cramped here. Mum, I can feel that you and Dad and my siblings can't wait to meet me now. I can feel and hear it when you say, "I love you, my sweet daughter". I can hear Dad's voice; he loves me now! I can hear my siblings too. They are very happy that they'll see me soon. I too can't wait to see you all, although I'm also very scared.

Mum, are you scared of labour? But why? You know how to give birth. Your body knows how to do it. My body also knows how to get out so that I can finally see you.

Mum, I can feel you calming yourself down. I like it so much when you're calm. I can be calm then, too. I'm so happy when you feel joyful and grateful. Be like that, then I can feel it all too. When it's like this, I am also well and calm. It's then that I trust you and believe that you'll be able to look after me and be just fine.

Mum, I'm ready to come into this world. I am you. You're ready and so I feel ready, too.

Mum, you're telling me more often that you love me and that you can't wait to meet me. This makes me feel all nice and warm. Talk to me like that as often as you can. It's also nice for you, and when you're feeling nice, so am I. Mum, I am you.

Mum, this is it. In just a short while, I'll be here. Be calm. You want me and I want you. I need you. Your love for me overfills me with joy.

THE BIRTH

Mum, for the last few hours my little home has been squeezing me and tightening around me. You've decided that it's time to go to the hospital. Dad's a little nervous but I can feel that he's there for you. We're not alone. **These contractions are not so bad either. Thanks to them, you'll get to see me and hug me soon enough.** One more push! Mum! I'm finally in your arms, snuggled into your chest. Mummy, this feels so good. I feel so safe when I can smell your scent, one I've known since the very beginning. I want to feel your heartbeat and be able to smell you. I know your voice, it's so soft and warm. I can hear you crying, full of emotions, telling me "I love you, my little treasure". Have I really moved you? Do you really love me? Do you really want me?

THE FIRST FEW *weeks in this world*

Mum, we're home! When I can hear that you're so happy about it, I am too. This is our home. It's where you feel safe and so I also feel safe.

Dad, I can feel your love for me, but why am I also feeling a certain anxiety towards you? I think it's these past situations that remind me that you didn't want me at first.

My siblings. Ah, they are so happy. But one of them isn't... why is he pushing me away? Why is he rejecting me? It's because he wants... well, what does he want? Mum didn't give him enough attention and now he feels rejected? And now he's mad at *me*? Why is he mad at me? I'm just a tiny little baby.

Dad, I can feel you loving me more and more. You're so happy that I'm a girl. You pick me up and take me into your arms more and more. It feels so nice and good. I can feel the warmth of your chest. It's so strong and soft; it feels so safe here. Daddy, protect me. Be my protection.

Mum, are you angry? At me? I can feel that you are, and I express this by crying. I don't know any other way.

Mum, did something scare you? What was it? Did you and Dad have a fight? Now I'm also scared. I'm scared. **You're scared and I am you, so I am also scared.**

Mum, I'm hungry. Feed me. Please. I'm crying because I'm hungry. Understand it. Feel it.

Mum, this milk from you is so delicious. It's so soothing, calming and reassuring. This moment when you're breastfeeding me and we're so close to each other is so wonderful.

Mum, touch me, play with me, talk to me, smile at me, be with me. I don't want to eat. Don't give me food. I want to feel your smell and touch. Take care of me. Look after me.

Mum, I like it so much when you stroke my head, my back, and my tummy. It's so wonderful. I love it when you care for me and give me your full attention. I can feel that you have true love for me. Pure, selfless, and unconditional love. Keep loving me like that and just the way I am.

I love you, my parents. I am made from you. I love you, my siblings. We are made from our parents. I love myself because I can love myself- it's healthy to love yourself."

This is how a child might express their emotions when they are first in the mother's womb and then after birth, when they are getting to know the world and their parents. In the following passage, I will show you examples from the lives of my clients who may have experienced such emotions at an early stage in their lives. For the purposes of this publication, their names and ages have been changed.

Examples from the conception period

Zofia, 34 years old:

I didn't want to have children. At least not now anyways. I was in a happy relationship, and we were both planning on having children someday. Yet all it took was a glass of wine or a beer for me to start making love to my husband and telling him to just finish inside me because I wanted to have children right there and then. Of course, I'm aware that alcohol relaxes you and may give you lots of weird and wonderful ideas, but I never wanted to make children drunk, even though that's the first thing that came to my mind after only a small amount. It was never thoughts about work, holidays, travelling or just simply good sex and a fun time; it was always to have children. How odd.

After talking with this client, it came out that her parents made her under the influence of alcohol. They were just at a party, nothing too crazy, and each had a couple glasses of wine. When the client found out about this and we both connected the dots, as well as used a technique which allows you to break your beliefs, she never found herself wanting children after drinking again. Coincidence? Maybe yes, maybe no...

PAULINA, **25 years old:**

I'm constantly embarrassed of myself. Embarrassed of the way I look, how I act, what I do. I'd rather hide and not show myself to anyone. I often curl up or slouch when I walk. I also blush often and would rather go unnoticed.

In the interview conducted, it became clear that the client was not a planned child. Her parents were young, they were 18 and 19 years old when my client's mother found out that she was pregnant. They enjoyed sex but were also ashamed of making love before marriage. On the one hand, her parents love united them, on the other hand, they felt internally embarrassed that they were committing a serious sin. This also made them feel ashamed of what they were doing. We focussed on regression therapy and during one of the sessions, my client felt the emotions present at the time of her conception, and the problem of her feeling constantly ashamed and embarrassed was alleviated.

EWA, **30 years old:**

> *Sex to me is something wonderful; the union of two souls. Conception is a miracle, and pregnancy is a blessed time. When my husband and I started trying for a baby, we tried to plan this as much as we could. We waited for the big day to come. When those two lines showed up on the pregnancy test, we celebrated, and the moment when our child was conceived was a magical one. Every single time we had sex brought us closer to having a child, and it was a wonderful, soulful event filled with ease.*

The client was a planned child, desired by her parents. Her mum fell pregnant very quickly and had a good pregnancy. Thanks to her mother, she was surrounded by positive beliefs about pregnancy, the time when you're trying for a baby, and childbirth. As a result, Ewa herself had very positive beliefs about sex, conception, pregnancy, and children. She came to me because of professional burnout. I always interview my clients about their lives to find the root cause of their problems. In this case, it's clear that the conception, or more precisely the emotional state of the parents, was positive and naturally translated into the life of Paulina.

Labour Begins in The Mind

Examples from the prenatal period

Ania, 30 years old:

> *When I meditate, I see my terrified pregnant mother. Her eyes are filled with fear. She's stood in the corner of the room grasping her belly. It feels as though she's scared of dad, and of what he might do or say. I think she's scared that he might hit her...*

After exploring this topic more, it became apparent that a previous pregnancy, which preceded my client's conception, had been terminated. What she saw and felt was her mother's emotional state, in which she was afraid of how her husband would react to the news of the unplanned pregnancy. In the case of the previous pregnancy, he had reacted with fear and anger, forcing his wife to get an abortion. Ania's mother recalled these emotions from the previous pregnancy, which in turn got coded into my client's body's memory, causing such images to appear during meditation.

KARINA, 33 years old:

> *I always feel incomplete, like I could just leave this world. Technically, everything's alright. I've seen everything, understood what I had to understand, I've lived, I've worked through my traumas... yet this indescribable feeling remains.*

It turned out that Karina had another trauma that she needed to work through. We discovered that the client's mother found out about the baby when she was four months pregnant and didn't manage to get an abortion in time. This moment was felt by the client as an agonising rejection, and this left a deep wound in her. Because of this wound, she constantly hesitates between life and death.

Example from the infancy period

Beata, 45 years old:

I constantly feel rejected. Men always reject me. I just can't build any happy and healthy relationship relationships with men, whether that be my boss rejecting me or something constantly going wrong in my private life. How long can a person cope with something like this?

Beata was frustrated that things were constantly going wrong in her life and that men kept abandoning her, both in a professional, as well as a private setting. After digging deeper into Beata's story, it turned out that when she was about three or four months old, she was left alone at home with her dad, who abandoned her emotionally. He got drunk and left the infant to fend for themself. This abandonment was so strong, that it later affected Beata's adult life.

IRENA, 41 years old:

> *I am always longing to feel secure. This is something that I have realised in my sessions. I work, I have a steady income, I am well educated and possess a lot of knowledge. I also have a partner that earns good money, yet I still have this constant fear and anxiety in me that something's going to happen or go wrong.*

From the memories of her infancy, Irena held onto a dark image in which she was alone. This triggered flashbacks that caused insecurity, fear, and anxiety. After becoming aware of this situation and making some adjustments, the sense of security returned.

BOŻENA, 21 years old:

> *I'm scared of shouting, particularly when it's coming from someone older than me. I don't run away because that's embarrassing but I do get scared, and my heart begins to race. I have no idea why I'm like this.*

When she looks back at her infancy, Bożena remembers most vividly moments when her parents were arguing. The shouting reminds her of those arguments. As a small child she felt threatened and unsafe, and this was still present in her adult body, making her react to these stimuli in the same way as she did when she was a child. As I have already mentioned at the beginning of this chapter, the time of conception is very important because life begins with it. This is something psychotherapist and psychology professor Anna Ancelin Schutzenberger from the University of Nice writes about in her book 'The Ancestor Syndrome: Transgenerational psychotherapy and the hidden links in the family tree'.

> *"The time of conception and what's going on in the parents' lives at this time is of great importance when it comes to understanding family life. Was the child wanted or not? Was it conceived out of love or as result of violence? Is the child meant to fix the relationship or replace a lost child? Is it a long-awaited boy after a series of girls? Or perhaps it was an accidental pregnancy that forced the parents to marry?"*

I've previously mentioned body memory and would like to quote an extract from the book "The Body Remembers: The Psychophysiology of Trauma and Trauma Treatment" by Babette Rothschild, a clinician with many years of experience: "understanding how the brain and body process, remember and consolidate traumatic events holds the key to healing the body and mind subjected to traumatic experiences"

And how is our present body any different from the one that has just begun being formed? Or how is our body different from that of an infant? Of course, there are some differences, but in the prenatal period and at the infancy stage, we are linked to our mother by a symbiotic bond that can be defined with the phrase 'I AM YOU'. **A child without a mother will not survive. In other words, I am you (the mother).** Many experts have written about this, one of them being John Bradshaw, an American psychologist. In his book 'Homecoming: Reclaiming and Championing your Inner Child', he writes: "we need a relationship with our mother, one that's caring and that we can copy. Infancy is called the symbiotic stage because we are absolutely dependent on the mother or the person taking care of our needs".

Qualified life counsellor and holistic therapist Susanne Hühn, writes about symbiosis in her book 'The Inner Child Workbook: What To Do With Your Past When It Just Won't Go Away' as follows: "In the womb you are totally dependent on your mother and her physical and mental abilities to provide for you. After birth, you take over the biological functions yourself, but you remain initially extremely dependent. You need a human being who consciously decides to take care of you, even when it is inconvenient to them; someone who is prepared be in a symbiosis with you. They must be able to listen to you, understand your needs, and even be able to sense these needs so that they can meet them. You are unaware of yourself, you are innocent. You need someone who responds to you positively and lovingly, someone who is happy to see you and care for you, someone who loves you. If you don't have someone like that, you can survive, but you cannot grow healthily, whether that be physically or emotionally. Love alone is not enough when the ability to care and provide is not there."

To finish, I would also like to mention a study which explains that **the baby feels everything that happens to the mother during the prenatal period and throughout infancy.** Pharmacology doctor Iliana Ramirez Rangel includes in her book, '*Częstotliwość serca*', various scientific studies on heart frequency and the possibility of regulating it yourself. She also explains how this frequency works between people. She writes "such strong synchronisation was also detected in mothers and their children. It turned out that the mother's brain waves (EEG-CZ) harmonised with her child's heartbeat (ECG), even though they had no physical contact with each other. All it took was for the mother to focus her attention on her child and her brain waves almost automatically synchronised with the baby's heartbeat".

Thus, we can conclude that the baby synchronises with the mother's emotions, whether that be anger, sadness, grief, peace, love, joy, or gratitude. Have you ever been in a situation where you've felt weird or upset because you were in a room where the atmosphere felt a bit on edge? Well, that's exactly it. You probably felt like that because you synchronised with your surroundings. The same thing happens to children, only more often and in a more intense way.

To summarise, a great deal of information is coded in the child's mind, or rather, in their body and conscience. I encourage everyone to be constantly giving their child unconditional love as it is vital for proper emotional, mental, and physical development.

It's important for the child to be exposed to positive and encouraging beliefs, feelings, emotions, and situations as often as possible. This will support them and positively foster their development at every stage and in the future, too. Don't forget to trust your child during pregnancy and labour. They know what to do. Focus on them, give them your attention and support, and look within yourself for limiting beliefs that hold you back. Maybe certain thoughts are not your thoughts and certain beliefs are not your beliefs. Maybe they come from your prenatal or infancy period? The answers are all within *you*. Open up to the knowledge and wisdom within *you*. This will lead you to happiness – not only that of your own but also your child's.

A space for your reflections.

Labour Begins in The Mind

---

1. Foetal heart monitor is also known as a Doppler.

2. "Following Hippocrates, the Greeks believed that the baby wants to be born. They said that at the end of the pregnancy, the child feels that their life-giving resources are running out. In order to save themself, they must escape from the cave in which they have been keeping themself safe in up until now. To do this, they begin to push with their feet in an attempt to pave their way to freedom." (F. Leboyer, "Birth without violence", p. 81).
3. During a workshop led by Olga, I was put into a trance and saw a mama bear with two young bears. The mama bear showed me the meaning of motherhood. I saw a happy little bear and a second, sad one. It was a picture of my children, and of me - as a mama bear.
4. What's this about us as souls choosing the parents to descend to? That's something spiritualists look at. If you are interested in this topic, I would recommend you check out the book Courageous Souls by Robert Schwartz.

Chapter 5
In the Older Sibling's Mind

It's not easy being a big sister. I had my parents all to myself until he came along. I was four years old when, on some random Friday in May, mum and dad went to the hospital and left me with my grandma. So supposedly, I knew that my brother was in my Mummy's belly, but let's be honest, what does four-year-old really know about any of that stuff anyway? My parents told me what I thought were interesting stories about what life with my little brother would be like, but they never mentioned the fact that at the beginning he would just eat and eat, and Mummy would just feed and feed, and that she wouldn't have any time for me at all. It was sad. Up until now, I would spend every second with my Mummy and now I had to share this time with him... but for what? I don't even need him anyways. I don't want a brother! Daddy, do something! I want to see my Mummy. Muuuum! Muuuum-myyyyy! Muuuuuuuuuuumm!

"WHAT DO YOU WANT?! **Can't you see I'm feeding the little one?" - I found myself losing my temper like that quite often because I didn't get the relevant support that I needed. Do** I regret it? Oh, very much so... I regret not being able to take care of myself. I regret that I was ashamed that I couldn't cope with breastfeeding. I regret **that I, mother hen, thought that I just HAD to manage somehow.** There are mothers out there who have several children- five, six, some even more- and survive. Me? I had two, yet I was struggling to cope with everything. My breasts hurt, I had plenty of breastmilk and the little one just kept crying and crying. I suffered with pain and despair, helplessness, and frustration, although not a single tear ran down my cheek because I was bottling up all my emotions. Kacper leeched onto my boob all day and all night long, and I stayed in bed with him, because that's where I was most comfortable feeding him. I didn't have time to go pee, eat or drink. Grzegorz was working. He had to. We couldn't afford to have any less money coming in because we were already struggling to make ends meet. All day I would just wait for him to get home.

"Mummy, will you play with me?"

"In just a second. I'll play with you when the little one finishes eating..."

———

MUM DOESN'T LOVE **me anymore. She prefers my brother.** She's constantly cuddling him and carrying him around. She doesn't have time for me anymore because he's here now. Why did they have to bring him home from the hospital? I didn't invite him here. I feel jealous and lonely...abandoned and unimportant. Dad where are you?! Why are you also never around anymore?

———

I HAVE tears in my eyes writing this. I still blame myself for not being able to take enough care of myself to also be there for my daughter. **This has taken a toll on our relationship, and I've been trying to rebuild it for years.** Even though things between us girls- or I should probably say 'us *women*' now- are much better (although having a teenage girl in the house is taking a lot more out of me than I thought it would), this jealousy in my daughter towards her brother remains, and it affects our whole family.

WHAT DO OLDER children need when another child comes into the family picture? **They want to be noticed, to feel important and needed. They want to belong to the family and be a fully-fledged member**. No matter how old your older child is, it's important to treat them with respect and let them be who they want to be. It's important to be there for them; to understand whatever it is that they're currently going through. It's also important to be able to see what's hidden deep inside them. Being there for them is just as important as accepting and noticing them.

AND SO, the years went by. I always tried to work jobs in which I could have my children next to me. I have a pedagogical qualification, so working with children posed no challenge to me and meant that I could have my Natalia right beside me. When I was pregnant with Kacper, I dressed up as a clown for a living, then I was a teacher and finally, the manager of a private nursery. **It was always possible for my children to be with me. But was it really that good for us?**

No, it wasn't. But just to be clear, that doesn't mean that it won't work for you and your family. For us it just simply didn't work- it was awful. Even though I had my children with me 24/7, it didn't feel like I really *had* them. I was too busy working with other children whilst my own beloved children were just right there next to me, watching. When I would get home after work, all I wanted was for them to go to bed because I was just too tired. I was exhausted and frustrated. I know now that that's not at all what motherhood is truly about.

Labour Begins in The Mind

It wasn't until we moved to the UK that I finally found the perfect balance. How ironic! Did I really have to move countries to be able to find it? As it turned out, it wasn't until we left Poland that I really felt the true responsibilities of being a mother. It doesn't mean that I took any less care of my children before, but here, in the UK, their fresh start in a new country and how their life would go here depended entirely on me and my husband. We were completely alone. In a new country, new culture, with a new language... my little ones only had us and each other now. I had to teach those same two kids that were always bickering and annoying each other that no matter the situation, they'll always have each other to count on, wherever they'll be and whatever they'll be doing.

Months passed. Natalia started primary school without any prior knowledge of English and Kacper stayed home with me. I was finally able to be there for them 24/7. For at least six hours every day when Natalia was in school, Kacper didn't have to share his mum with his older sister. I noticed a change in their relationship. Fortunately, it was a positive one. They were experiencing so many changes in their lives, not only changes to their surroundings but also changes in their parents. Mum was no longer so tired all the time, had a big smile on her face, and was more willing to play, go for a walk or to the park.

Mum had time. Children see parents giving them time as a way of showing them that they love them. To them, time is just another part of love. Individual time for each child in the family is important.

And contrary to what it may seem like, the more children, the more love, and more time... BECAUSE LOVE MULTIPLIES

WHEN IT IS SHARED. Every morning we woke up with smiles on our faces after a good night's sleep. How? Because we slept close to each other. We still sleep together, although we don't do it every night anymore. We sleep like this every time we need it or just whenever when we can. Back then, the housing situation played a big role in the way that we slept. I didn't realise that our children feel so much calmer when they sleep with us. It's also a lot warmer because everyone's cuddling and keeping each other warm. It was feeling safe and physically close to each other that allowed us to wake up each morning with a smile on our face. Our days were filled with feelings of security and closeness, and we quickly fell into a routine of life in the UK. It was then that we started looking for a bigger place for the four of us.

We found a house where everybody could have their own bedroom. Does having your own room affect family relationships? Yes, it does. It affects the relationships both positively and negatively. A good thing about living in a big house is that you have more space to store unnecessary crap. And the bad thing? You're all far away from each other, you talk less, sit alone in your room, and live in your own world.

You're probably wondering what any of this has to do with this chapter. What does any of this have to do with creating a positive image of childbirth for your older kids? Well let me tell you...

> *The bonds we build within the family influence the way in which the older children will welcome the new family member.*

The closer the family bonds are, the more easily and openly the older sibling will welcome the newborn. Preparing children for the arrival of another child in the family is quite a challenge. A whole multitude of questions appear: "where do babies come from?", "how did she get in your belly, Mummy?", "how is she going to get out of there?". As parents, we have to face them and answer them truthfully, with biology, but gently enough so that the child understands what we want to tell them. We have to do it in a way that's appropriate to their development stage and cognitive abilities. Children have a right to know how they came into this world. Let go of that old tale about storks.... Seriously! **Words like sperm and egg cell should be treated the same as an arm, a leg, or a butt.** They are parts of our bodies too! If they weren't there, you wouldn't even be here! There are children who will enquire in detail, like our Natalia did, and others who will say, "I hope it's a girl because then I won't have to share my toys", like our Kacper.

You've probably noticed by now that I've been using 'she' pronouns when talking about another baby. You'll remember from the first chapter that I miscarried a pregnancy. Although we didn't know the gender, my heart told me that it was a boy. Shortly after this happened, my womb became a home to Patrycja. And so now it was time to prepare the two older siblings for Patrycja's homebirth. To prepare well for a family birth, it's necessary to tell your child what it's going to look like. It's best that this is done during the pregnancy or even earlier, when you're not pregnant yet but planning to be. This will facilitate the arrival of the sibling, so that it doesn't cause jealousy or come as a sudden surprise.

Many couples ask me why our older children were with us when I gave birth to Patrycja, or why I didn't organise childcare for them. After all, childbirth is not something for children to see.

And my answer is always this:
  Give the older child the choice of whether they want to be present at birth, or maybe they only want to be present

> *up to a certain point. Acknowledge that they are a full participant in the birth and a full-fledged member of your family. Always treat them seriously and with respect.*

In any planned family birth, it's important to make sure you have someone ready who'll be able to look after them in case something goes wrong, or perhaps in case the child decides that it no longer wants to be there. You can also have their favourite movies or cartoons ready for them in another room.

If you don't have anyone to help, you can hire a doula. They will certainly take good care of the older siblings (and household pets, too!). The participation of older siblings in the birth process should also be included in the BIRTH PLAN and given to the midwife. The midwife should also prepare for the fact that there will be other people present at birth.

Usually when older kids are asked where children are born, their answer would be 'at the hospital'.

> *I felt a huge responsibility but, at the same time, I was also proud to show them what a natural birth looks like, and I was proud to be able to see how it affects the relationship between siblings.*

What happened next caught me off guard. I didn't see it coming and wouldn't think that it could happen, not even in my wildest dreams. **Neither of my older children were jealous of Patrycja**. They happily welcomed her into their circle without even batting an eye. They both witnessed the birth of a younger sister, so there was no element of surprise. It wasn't as if mum had gone to the hospital with a big belly and just came back with a baby. This time, they were able to observe, accompany, support, experience, feel – they were able to just *be* there. And so, the puzzle solved itself: storks don't bring babies, nor do they come from a magical baby factory that's somewhere high up in the clouds, and as it turned out, the doctor doesn't always pull the baby out from mummy's belly.

AGNIESZKA PLUTA-SZKARADEK

Most of the children I've had the pleasure of talking to about childbirth told a similar story. This story resembled the description of a caesarean section: "Mum goes to the hospital, the doctor opens up her belly, pulls the baby out and that's it". Children's imagination stems from what they hear about birth from those around them. They might hear something without you realising it, or maybe you've said something accidentally when they were around; it doesn't necessarily have to be from a specific conversation. It's enough for us adults to talk to someone about birth, and if the children are in the room and you say something like "cover your ears, this conversation is not for children", you can be just about 100% sure that those ears will hear everything. **Therefore, the way we talk about childbirth has a big influence on how children perceive birth.**

Since the beginning of my pregnancy with Patrycja, we held conversations in our house about her being born in a pool, in the water, and at home. Yes, you read that right- at home. The whole pregnancy was natural, and so the birth was too. Thanks to this, I gave my daughter the most beautiful gift a mother can give to a growing girl: I showed her that childbirth can be a beautiful experience and the way we perceive it is very likely to influence its course.

Opening your heart up to every contraction opens up the body and helps you give birth.

As you prepare your older child for this amazing family celebration, try to show them everything as best as you can; describe, illustrate, and show on Youtube what might happen during birth. Prepare them for the sounds they might hear and reassure them that it's natural and necessary for mums to do that, and that nothing bad is happening, even when mummy is screaming.

Make your child an active participant in the birth. They could, for example, bring you something to drink, something to eat, turn on some music or dim the lights. A big brother or sister can even fulfil themselves as photographers. A younger child can paint animals that they associate with their mum as she gives birth. This will help distract them from the loud noises and will also encourage them to play an active role in the birth. **Children have a natural curiosity about the world, so let's help them develop it, not only during childhood, but also throughout their whole lives.**

When the special day arrived, our children were one hundred percent prepared. Kacper had been asked several times beforehand if he wanted to go to his aunt's, and he told us that he did. Natalia knew straight away that she wanted to accompany me until the very end. As you'll already know from the first chapter, I went into labour at night, so I didn't wake anyone up. Grzegorz was at work, and it wasn't until he came back that we turned on the light and vacuumed the living room (at 3am!). I did the dishes that I couldn't be bothered to do them the night before, and then started highlighting my BIRTH PLAN. Before the labour started, I remember thinking that I "still have time", even though I had just gone into my 42nd week of pregnancy. My colourful birth plan was proudly displayed on the wall, and it took up so much of the wall, that it caught Natalia by surprise in the morning.

As the pool filled up, my eldest little joy quickly swapped her pyjamas for a swimsuit and jumped into the water. I didn't feel the need to use it just yet. I don't know if you remember me telling you that these contractions were pleasant, joyful, gentle, and effective ones all at the same time. Meanwhile, I kept waiting for the kind of contractions I remember having when giving birth to Kacper-

Labour Begins in The Mind

awfully strong ones that just straight up knocked me off my feet. There were none of those this time around and thanks to this, the image of a natural birth will be the most beautiful childhood memory I could give my children. It will be the most beautiful memory to my daughter, because she, too, will become a mum one day (I hope so, anyway), and to my son, because he will be a wonderful dad (I can feel it in my bones).

It was a wonderful night. Our children's reaction was beautiful:

At 8am, Kacper came into the room, still half-asleep because he got woken up by noises. A little irritated, he announced that I was 'disturbing' his play, and then off he went into another room, totally engrossed by his Lego. Natalia was still close by, keeping guard. When I gave birth to Patrycja, my eldest looked at me and with a beaming smile on her face, she exclaimed "She's beautiful! She looks just like Kacper when he was this tiny. Thank you, Mum."

"Where's Kacper?" I asked, looking around the room, slightly surprised that he wasn't there yet. "Can you call him over, please?".

Kacper came down to the living room a little reluctantly.

"This is your new little sister."

Kacper didn't speak at first. He ran out into the garden in his pyjamas and returned a moment later with a tiny bouquet of wildflowers.

"Mummy, thank you for giving birth to such a lovely little girl! At least she won't take my toys away from me", he remarked.

Natalia looked at Patrycja, already eager to hold her in her arms. After she proudly cut the umbilical cord, it was time for the little sisters' first interaction.

"Hello, Patrycja. I'm Natalia, your new best friend. From now on we will play together, and I will look after you because I am your big sister."

SO, **what does childbirth look like in the eyes of the older siblings? Exactly as we portray it to them**. Older children who have been prepared for this moment will be the perfect companions. If they understand what's going on around them, then their role will prove to be invaluable. And if they're smaller children, they're certainly still very empathetic and will sense what it's all about.

> *The homebirth brought our older children closer to Patrycja, bringing practically no change to their home routine. I was not sick; I was not in hospital. It turned out that when a child is born at home, the problems associated with feeling rejected and not understanding 'where the child came from' just simply does not exist.*

From day one, Natalia has been able to cradle Patrycja in her arms, helping change her and caring for the little one. "The way a woman gives birth has an impact on the rest of her life. How can you think that it doesn't matter? Unless you think a woman doesn't matter either." (B. Beech, B. Phipps).

The birth of our youngest daughter was a joyous family celebration in which the older children participated. They did not associate the birth with being separated from their mum or with the fact that mum looks like she's seriously ill. Natalia says that she now knows what childbirth can look like, and that she cannot imagine giving birth in hospital. The birth of a child has become something natural for them. I have already mentioned several times in this book that childbirth is a natural, physiological act and as such requires no special assistance if the pregnancy has gone well. I've also already told you that our midwives did not arrive in time and knocked on the door just as I was already getting out of the pool with the newborn in my arms. However, knowing that I was surrounded by people who I trust, love and who are my whole entire world, I felt safe and calm.

I was blessed with incredible intimacy during Patrycja's birth. It's exactly what I needed but unfortunately lacked the last time I gave birth.

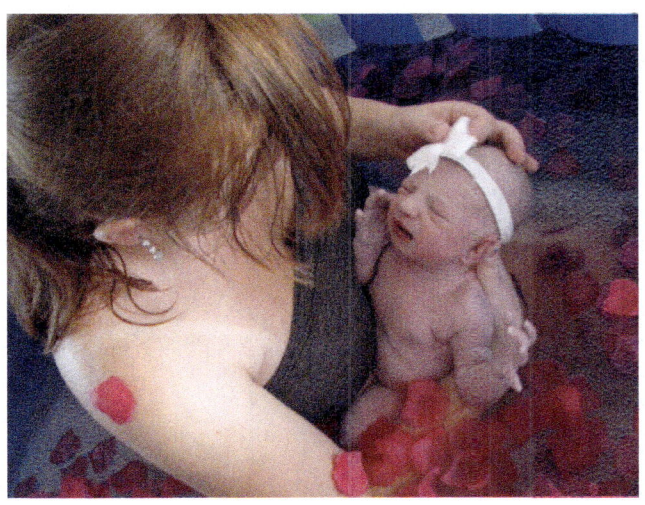

A space for your reflections.

AGNIESZKA PLUTA-SZKARADEK

In Your Mum's, Mother-in-Law's, Grandma's, Auntie's, and Neighbour's Mind

... or in other words, how to deal with the opinions of those who do not fully understand your thoughts on what a birth should look like, and who do not respect your choices.

I would like to begin this chapter with an appeal:

Take the matter of childbirth into your own hands. Be responsible for yourself and your child. Don't many any decisions that aren't in agreement with what YOU want.

Let me tell you about the history of obstetrics. I'll tell you about what's been done to women over many years and how they were cleverly made to believe that they were incapable of giving birth without needing highly skilled medics. And we, children of the 80s and the 90s, are the unlucky inheritors of this. It's up to us to determine how the next generation views childbirth.

Jennifer Worth brilliantly portrays these changes of the maternity care system in her book 'Call the Midwife', but the series adaptation of the book portrays these even better. The series emphasises just how much the people involved in the women's labour affect her behaviour. It also illustrates how the women's views on childbirth affect the birth, the pain she feels, and any possible complications. We can also easily point out the moment in which natural homebirths 'transitioned' to hospital births, which were more medicalised and- and I'm saying this both metaphorically and ironically- 'luxurious'. After the Second World War, with the development of state health services, women began to be shown beautiful, clean, hygienic hospitals which were meant to be this ideal place to give birth to their child. This concept came from the West, where medicine was developing faster than in Eastern Europe. Unfortunately, these same medical developments have led the US to having one of the highest percentages of maternal and neonatal mortality in the world. What's more, almost half of the births end in a caesarean[1]. Such lies made women want to give birth in a hospital where she would be alone, without her partner, and lying flat with their legs strapped to cold metal racks.

Seriously?? Have we really allowed them to experiment on us, *women*, just because it was more comfortable for the doctors? And now, the biggest problem- the medicalisation of births. Births have lost their individuality, become just another statistic, and now have to happen within a certain timeframe and with a multitude of medical interventions. They fell into the hands of doctors who were (and still are) predominantly men. I'm sorry gentlemen, I've got nothing against you, but how can a man understand what a woman in labour is going through?? Not only this, but midwives were pushed aside and became more of a birthing assistant than a midwife. Worse still, **women were made to believe that homebirths are dangerous and in Poland they were actually temporarily illegal.** Thus was born a generation of 30-something-year-olds who now demand a c-section and believe that they're entitled to one.

My apologies, it seems I got carried away with my emotions... let's get back on track.

I believe that thinking positively about childbirth is an absolute must. The negative beliefs we've had drilled into us since childhood by mothers, aunts, friends, friends of friends, films, and other forms of mass media, have done nothing but cut us off from our own desires and natural instincts.

Because I was aware of the physiological processes going on in my body (and after all, childbirth is a perfectly physiological phenomenon, although these days it is treated as if it were a serious illness), we decided to share our idea to give birth at home with our closest family.

I associate illness with being forced to stay in some sort of medical facility, like a treatment centre or a hospital, and lots of tests. As a child, I was very afraid of having my blood drawn. I was SO scared! I remember this one time when I had to go by myself to get my blood drawn. I don't know why my mum or dad couldn't come with me, but I remember that I was about 11 years old, and that I knew one of the nurses working at the clinic. The nurse's name was Renata and I remember that when she was preparing the equipment, something in me clicked. I started shouting that I didn't want it, that I didn't agree, that I would come back another time with my mum... In the end I ran away. Now I understand that I just really needed to have someone there with me. When I fell pregnant for the first time (actually, the second time too), I realised just how much the feelings of abandonment and of being left alone stuck with me. It's no wonder that those births turned out the way they did...

I started asking myself how the hell I was supposed survive a birth if I couldn't even go get my blood drawn because it scared me too much. You already know all about my transformation journey from the previous chapters you've read.

I had to explain to this little child, who had curled into a little ball from fear, hiding somewhere in the depths of my subconscious, that getting my blood drawn was nothing and that it hardly hurt. What really hurts us, is our own fear. Luckily, the thing with fear is that once you've conquered it once, it's always easier the next time around.

Michel Odent identified two key factors to a successful birth: **there needs to be a sense of *safety* as well as a sense of *intimacy* in the woman.** In my case, these two components could only exist in the privacy of my own home. I firmly believe that it's thanks to the fact that I had to explain to everyone why I wanted to have a natural birth and share the story of why it will be so beautiful, that I have managed to effectively change my negative beliefs about birth once and for all. I was finally able to paint a new picture of childbirth for myself. I am also convinced that a homebirth is the most natural and most primitive form of bringing a child into this world. To top it all off, it's also the most 'ecological' and 'budget friendly' way.

For the first time in my life, I could face the conversation about my desires for a homebirth with people who tried to talk me out of it. I did it calmly, boldly and with a smile, even when they tried to force me to choose the hospital instead. There came a point when certain members of my family started asking if I had already packed my hospital bag, where our older children would be during the birth, and how we would manage to do it all alone... it was time to break the big news to them. Their reactions varied. They ranged from "okay, fine, but if anything happens, you're going to go to the hospital, right?", to ones that made me regret even saying anything in the first place. From the day my mother and sister found out about our little plan, I began receiving regular phone calls from them as they invented more and more reasons for why I should give up on this 'crazy, irresponsible, immature and just plain stupid idea', and why in their opinion I should go to the hospital instead, where it's 'safe'. Trying to talk to them didn't help and I felt like my mother wasn't at all listening to what I had to say. I felt sad that she couldn't just respect my decision.

To her, it was safer to give birth in a hospital, but for me, it was at home. **The woman must ask herself where she'll feel**

more comfortable and which place will make her feel safer.

Labour Begins in The Mind

I am strong, I am powerful!

Put everything you've ever heard about pregnancy and childbirth into a big bag. Throw in there everything you've heard about breastfeeding, the way we should raise our children, how they should sleep, how we should carry them, feed them, or play with them. Throw it all in, tie the bag and chuck it out the window. **Forget all the information they tried to feed you with until now.**

In the 70s, 80s and 90s, many families were deprived of deeper relationships and bonds. It was a time when our mothers were told that the baby had to sleep alone in the cot, that they were not allowed to carry the baby because it would get used to it, and that it could be given fennel tea and a carrot when it was three months old. This was a time when there was no breastfeeding support and milk-like powders (which today we call modified milk) appeared from the West. And unsurprisingly enough, they sold well; maternity leave was short, mothers went back to work and the baby had to be fed with something.

Fortunately, today we're living in much better times. And even though we may be struggling a little bit financially, I put my family and the relationship we have with each other above all else, because that's something they won't teach the kids in school. Instead, they will learn many other things that aren't very useful in life, and as adults, they'll find themselves questioning it all. School won't teach them about a woman's menstrual cycle and how you can calculate it, nor will they teach them about how beautiful a pregnancy is or that the child knows how to be born, and that the mother is the child's companion during this beautiful time. Dad is mum's companion, and the midwife is the parents' companion. Sometimes there's also me, the doula. I try to be the best companion I can be to everyone.

It'd be great to know how to deal with those people that have a completely different opinions about birth, and about the way that we choose to lead our lives. I'm not going to try and be original here- the best solution is to just *talk*. Remember though, it has to be a dialogue, not a monologue. It's not about spilling out all our thoughts and feelings, instead, it's about empathetically listening to each other and trying to understand what the other person has to say. When we talk about childbirth, are we both thinking of the same shade of 'brown'? (Thanks, Izabela Antosiewicz, this is a useful piece of advice that really helps during conversations[2]).

Next, think about the way in which you express yourself. Are your facial expressions, gestures and tone of voice effectively conveying what it is that you wish to say? Do you immediately go into 'defence mode'? Maybe to avoid feeling hurt, it's you that attacks first?

I often did that. I was so afraid of rejection and of people proving me that I was inferior, weaker, or nothing, that, instead of talking, I let my 'attack mode' take over. I always made sure to stand my ground, even when I knew that I was in the wrong. I was so afraid of failure that I never gave up. Fortunately, if we really want to, we can learn to control ourselves.

Working on yourself leaves you feeling fulfilled, so I would encourage you to do so. Maybe not right now, today, or right away, because some things take time, but finding the cause of your fears, anxiety and behaviour is truly worth it. Our behaviour stems from somewhere, there's always a reason behind it. Sometimes it's to do with the way you were born, other times it's to do with the relationships in your family home. It is worth finding out why you are the that way you are. Just being aware of it is helpful, and just you wait how great it will be when you finally work through it! This skill will come in handy when having conversations with your doctors, midwives, family, and friends who you may find that you don't always see eye to eye with.

Have you ever wondered just what the difference is between

an obstetrician and a midwife? The best definition I've managed to find was in Irena Chołuj's book *'Urodzić razem i naturalnie'*. She writes that **"an obstetrician is a specialist in high-risk labours and the midwife is a specialist in natural labours". I would also just like to add that women are also specialists in natural labours.**

If your doctor or midwife does not support your approach to childbirth, remember that you can always entrust the management of your pregnancy with someone who will support you. It may also be worth considering stopping or limiting contact with the people who cause confusion. However, this would be better to do just whilst you're pregnant, as it's not beneficial in the long run. I believe that problems are better solved than just swept under the carpet. Furthermore, I come from a generation whose parents fixed something if it was broken, rather than putting it aside or throwing it away. I won't give you any ready-made solutions because I don't have any of those. Not everything that's worked for me is necessarily going to work for you. However, the principle for both of us is the same: an honest conversation with well-structured arguments, preferably based on EBM (or in other words, Evidence Based Medicine).

And so go! Gather knowledge, read, look, talk, and trust yourself and your intuition. Your heart will never let you down. Reason can sometimes be confused by the amount of information it's given, but the heart always knows best.

I invited a psychologist to write the last chapter because I believe that pregnancy, childbirth, and early motherhood bring many changes that are worth looking at with a specialist's eye. A psychologist is someone who will not only help and advise you but will also, above all, listen and understand. My aim was not only to revise my knowledge of childbirth, but also to ensure that I pass it on to you in a reliable way. I dedicate this next chapter to myself because I still have a lot of room for improvement when it comes to relationships with myself and with others. I demand a lot from myself, and the more I learn, the more I demand. I'm not yet at the stage I dream of being at, but that's why I trust that with the next chapter, we will learn to look at pregnancy, childbirth, and interpersonal relationships in a new way. It will be a challenge for us.

Let us begin to build the world anew. Let the new generations know what love, acceptance, respect, safety, and support is.

A space for your thoughts and reflections.

1. Based on the film 'The Business of Being Born', https://www.youtube.com/watch?v=7lxbES6xzfM, accessed on 27.01.2021
2. You can find out exactly what this brown thing is all about in Izabela Antosiewicz's book "*Nakarm, naucz i puść wolno*".

Chapter 7
In the Psychologist's Mind

My name is Agnieszka Michalska. I am a psychologist, but also a woman and a mother. It's with great interest that I read the previous chapters. I was very impressed by them, and I appreciate the degree of honesty and openness, as well as the author's willingness to share her experience with the reader of a non-invasive, natural childbirth.

The fact that childbirth can be natural, peaceful, non-medical, and we could even say, an 'ordinary' or 'everyday' event, is hardly spoken of. In fact, it's as though we're not even allowed to think about it in that way. Our culture takes away women's power by frightening us into thinking that we cannot manage without doctors. What's more, they fail to mention that we're the main characters, the subjects, and not just someone that gets treated as an object during labour. The woman should be able to have a say in this whole situation; in the process, in what happens to her, where she gives birth, how she gives birth and of course, who is with her.

Simply reading this book is not enough, although it is an important and valuable start. Preparation is key. You need to give yourself time to get closer to yourself and to your idea of childbirth, as well as to the fears you may hold about it, and your hopes. You need to make a birth plan and know your rights.

Pregnancy naturally is and should be a time of serenity; a moment to slow down and to listen to yourself. If we rush through life with a notebook full of to-do lists and a head full of plans that are always shifting and running away from us, we are not helping ourselves. It's worthwhile and absolutely essential to meet our basic needs: to have a home

Labour Begins in The Mind

(whether it's your own or rented), one in which we feel safe, to have finances secured or to have a plan for how to secure these finances so that you don't have to leave your newborn or infant in the care of someone else. At the beginning, this will do. It goes without saying that a basic layette needs to be prepared, and here I recommend consulting a sensible mum who already knows what's necessary and what's crucial before consulting magazines, internet articles or God forbid, social media. They just want to get money from us, rather than caring for our well-being. At the end of this book, you'll find a list of good sources to turn to.

When a woman finds out that she's pregnant, no matter how she reacts, she usually knows straight away that this baby will now become the single most important thing in her world, especially if it's her first pregnancy. She starts planning what their room's going to look like, their little corner and their cot. She knows that she will meet the little one's every need, and she ponders of what she'll need to do to achieve this. She imagines how wonderfully she'll take care of her newborn, and even if she is sometimes scared, she believes that she's a great mum– the best one out there– convinced that she'll never let her baby down.

Ah, so many ideas fill her mind. Unrealistic ones, may I add.

Do you remember that thing the air hostess always tells us when we're on the plane? That if the air pressure ever goes down, we must first fit our own mask before fitting our child's'? Well, it's an important and sensible safety procedure, but also a great metaphor for parenting and motherhood.

So why am I writing about all this anyway? Well, because **sometimes it's hard. In fact, it's like that quite often. Sometimes it gets a little easier but it's often unbearable.** All the responsibilities, the sleepless nights, troubles with breastfeeding, the worry that you've overfed your baby or maybe not fed it enough, the so-called 'colic'[1], later comes the teething, and Heaven forbid you try living up to all those 'perfect' mums from Instagram. And to top it all off, you've got the aunties, uncles, grandparents, and neighbours popping in to see the baby, but completely forgetting about the mother and her needs.

You see, if you've not yet learned by now how to meet your needs and you're still trying to be the best at everything you do, you're in for a real fast-track course on assertiveness. If you skip out on it, then unfortunately you're going to have to pay a huge price, both mentally and physically.

I'm sorry to say this, but if this is the case, then your child may also emotionally suffer. **So, now that you're pregnant, PUT YOURSELF FIRST**. I'm serious. Are you the only one who cooks at home, does the dishes, and does the shopping? Or maybe you're the best at cleaning and doing the laundry? Is your partner great at getting away with not doing the chores? Or maybe he only does them when you remind him to do so? All these activities take up a lot of time. So much time that now you take for granted but that you simply just won't have when the baby finally comes. If you don't start being assertive and getting your partner to share the responsibility of household chores with you now, then you may find yourself in a big crisis soon.

Let me say it again: when you start looking after your little one, you won't have the time anymore to cook, clean, or do the laundry. After birth, your hormones will be buzzing and everything will be difficult: you'll have an aching body, a huge responsibility, sore breasts - and these are just some examples of the difficulties that will arise. **Believe me, the last thing you need are the expectations of a of a man who, on his return from**

work and with two left hands for household chores, expects everything to be tidied up and to have a hot dinner on the table waiting for him, because, after all, you don't have to go to work…

Even if your partner doesn't expect this of you but it's you who has such ideas and expectations about your life, I would advise you to change these quickly. Otherwise, you'll end up frustrated and not only with a cluttered and messy home, but worse still, with a cluttered heart and mind.

Your priorities will be to look after your needs and your child's needs. That's it.

This is not the time to put the needs of others above your own and your child's because you will no longer have any energy left for that. Simply speaking, you're already doing enough and can't be doing any more than you already are. **A mature partner will understand this and will do everything they can to take over many of the responsibilities at home.** I would encourage you to prepare yourself strategically for this moment and to start getting your partner used to the idea that it will now be them who will have to take care of the house and do it at least half as well as you do.

A note from the author

Allow me to make a small digression here. As the author of this book, I feel that my words may sometimes be misunderstood. I don't mean to present the roles of men and women in a stereotypical manner. Please try to find the meaning in our words and understand what we're trying to convey.

Dear men, if you are reading this passage, know that what I want to tell you comes mainly from my experience of working as a doula with different couples. I know how hard you work to provide for your family, and I appreciate your professional efforts. I would also encourage you to commit yourself to caring for your child and to raising them. It's very important for you to be a support during this challenging time. A child needs his mother and father as role models from the very beginning. As you probably know, children learn by observing and then copying adult behaviour. And although you may think that a newborn baby doesn't yet imitate anything, believe me when I tell you that they feel everything. They feel both your emotions and your partner's, and they fully absorb all of it.

EVERYONE ALWAYS TOLD me that all newborns do is eat and sleep. Yet nobody told me what an effect these essential needs would have on me and my partner. My baby was 'unputdownable'. My daughter literally lived on me and every attempt to put her down, even for a minute, whether that was during the day or night, ended in crying. **As a psychologist, I knew that meeting her emotional needs would build an underlying sense of security, and that over time, she would become less and less dependent on us and more confident.** I knew what I had to do, but I found it very difficult at times. **I couldn't do anything other than take care of my child.**

The baby wrap was my salvation. I took a babywearing class led by a professional advisor when my baby was two months old. Because Pola was born premature, we had to wait until then. She was too small to put in a wrap sooner as it could've been dangerous for her. The wrap made it possible for me to do other things than just cuddle my daughter-I was finally able to free my hands. I could make myself a cup of tea or cut up some veggies for a salad. In fact, it's even how we decorated our Christmas tree!

As I write this chapter, Pola is 20 months old. She's an adorable, joyful baby who really likes to cuddle. Sometimes she doesn't want to leave our arms, but when she's feeling good, well rested and full, she's happy to take care of herself and can play on her own for a longer period of time. I am writing this so that you are prepared; so that you're both ready for everything. I want to make sure that you're ready for the difficult moments too, and perhaps above all, so that you're ready for the most difficult ones. Know that your life will also be filled with wonderful, moving moments. There will certainly be many of those! These, however, do not require any special precautions.

How a newborn or infant is treated is hugely important in the development of their brain and emotionality. It influences the kind of child they will be, as well as the kind of adult.

A note from the author

Psychologist Agnieszka Michalska's words focus mainly on the mother, her feelings, and her emotions. This was the aim of this chapter-**MAMA COMES FIRST**. However, the family model I write about throughout this book is about a man, a woman, and a child (or children). In this model, the family is its own unit that makes a whole; one that completes, supports and loves each other, as well as being respectful and accepting.

Dear Woman, after the birth of your child, put yourself and your little one first and make sure that you keep it this way for a long time. "How long?", I hear you ask. That depends on you and only you. Shortly after the birth, everything else will fall into second place. YOU, your partner, and your child are most important. You are the ones who make up the family. During this time, a high amount of prolactin lowers your libido and will make sure that you are a mother first and foremost, but the relationship with your husband is most important. It's you guys that form the basis of a successful, happy family. It's in you that all the good you'll pass onto your children lies. I know, I know...it's all very difficult and demanding, but it is definitely doable.

In this part of the book, the author of the chapter talks about the mother-child relationship, but that does not mean that the man is not there or that he is less important. Dear Dad, you are a very important piece in this puzzle. Without you, this puzzle wouldn't make any sense. Trust your woman and child, be close to them, surround them with love and care, and let them lean on your strong shoulder whenever they need to. Don't forget that you are the rock of this family. In this chapter, we're trying to explain that the postpartum stage is a time which takes a reality of its own and that it's only temporary. Therefore, understanding what's going on in the woman's head and in her body (and by that, I mean her hormones) will enable you to feel accepted, important and needed...even if, from time to time, she may throw around words like "leave me alone!". I would like for you too, Dad, to remember your needs and your emotions because postpartum affects you as much as it does Mum. In fact, postnatal depression can also affect fathers. If you ever feel that you need some support, don't be ashamed to seek professional help. Do it not only for yourself, but above all, do it for your family.

I'm a big promoter of attachment parenting, and I also believe that all that's natural is best.

Labour Begins in The Mind

Breastfeeding, cuddling your child as soon as it starts crying, responding to the baby's needs right away, sleeping with the baby in the family bed, and being there for them whenever they show that they need it-all of this is natural and good for the baby. It's also often easier for the mum. This stage is necessary and it's not only important that the man consents to this way of raising the child, but it's also important that he actively participates in household chores and supports the woman in every step of the way.

When I hear stories about how someone's child sleeps so wonderfully in a separate room, and that it only took a few times of leaving the child alone in a room until it eventually stopped crying, I feel extreme objection. I am very much against this kind of practice and find it difficult to understand how little empathy you must have towards your own child to treat it this way. They get terrified and learn that when they cry no one will come to their rescue, not even their own mother. What a terrible world it must be if no one wants to help a little one. The child learns that crying does not help and learns not to cry so that they can save their energy for later. Exhausted by this tiring despair, and with hugely elevated levels of the stress hormone cortisol, the child finally falls asleep. Cortisol and stress change the structures of the brain in a way that causes the child to never be as calm, trusting, and cheerful as they might have been had it not been for this traumatic experience. So, if you are a mother or a father and someone advises you to train your child to fall asleep in such a bestial way, don't listen to them and know that this person's advice is worthless, as well as unimaginably harmful.

And believe me, you'll be getting a lot of advice about anything and everything from everyone- your mum, mother-in-law, sister, friends, colleagues, neighbour.... You'll get it all throughout your pregnancy, before you get pregnant, right before you give birth and after you give birth, too.

> *If you love your child deeply, then you know exactly what they need. You also know that it's you who they need the most. Please be as emotionally available to them as much as they need you to be.*

Don't let your child 'cry it out' either. This is another awful piece of advice that brings terrible consequences. You might hear some say "hey, little children cry, it's normal", but I don't agree. You can't just let a baby cry and tell them to calm down on their own. Instead, the baby needs to be cuddled by a calm adult, and long enough for them to stop crying. If the crying comes back because, for example, the mother put the baby down again, then this is a sign that the baby wants to be close. As parents, what we should do is be there for them and be with him until they calm down and feel sure that they're safe.

Today, we've got the whole internet and so many specialists at the reach of our fingertips. Are you interested in how your child is developing physiologically? Well then have a look on the internet for a good physiotherapist, give them a call and make an appointment for a consultation. Do you have lactation problems or don't know when to introduce other foods into your child's diet? The same principle applies – have a little look for specialists and get in contact with them.

> *Don't listen to the advice of other women, and certainly don't listen to them when you feel that your intuition is telling you that 'you're going about things in the wrong*

way'. When you feel like your heart is breaking because you're doing something against yourself to help your child, and you can see that they're crying and trying to tell you that they're suffering, then trust me, you're definitely going about things in the wrong way.

This is bad for you, your child, and the relationship you have with them.

If we all still lived in caves, then nobody would ever doubt the fact that the baby should sleep next to their parents or that they should be carried close to them-or else they run the risk of getting eaten alive by something. It's no different today and children still only feel safe when next to us. Even if we think that we are modern people, with gadgets such as bedside cribs, baby monitors, bottles, and baby formulas, all of which we have no problems using...

This still doesn't change the fact that our bodies, and above all, our nervous systems and emotional needs haven't changed for thousands of years.

Newborns don't know that it's already the 21st Century and so they won't be able to meet today's expectations of being so independent from day one. **Please, be as close to your children as they need you to be and listen to them; they will surely let you know when they are ready for different changes like sleeping in separate rooms.** When the time comes, I assure you that they will let you know.

Follow your child's needs, don't impose what you think are

solutions on them, and don't think that crying is a natural state for him. On the contrary, it must be prevented as quickly and as effectively as possible. With this approach, your relationship will strengthen, and the child will not lose confidence in you and the world around them. They will feel safe, and you will feel that you understand them better and that you know how to communicate with them instead of fighting them.

If you find yourself in a situation in which those closest and dearest to you fail to support you and disapprove of your choices in a homebirth, breastfeeding, co-sleeping or even baby wrap wearing, then you must remember to trust yourself and to be resistant. **Let those people go and don't expect them to support you; absolutely do not waste your energy and time trying to convince them about your choices.** It is best to just cut off the conversation by saying "it's my life, my pregnancy" and then, "my baby and my choices. You can agree or disagree with me, but it won't affect me or my decision". If someone takes offence- tough! At least you'll get a break from all that intrusive advice. It's worth taking care of yourself in such a situation, and if they don't take offence, add "and if you really want to help me because you are worried about us, then..." - and you may wish to suggest "you could do my shopping or mop the floor because I can't cope. Maybe you could take a few days off after I give birth and be there for me when my partner goes back to work". These types of needs will really need to be met.

Labour Begins in The Mind

I have got feminine power

In my experience, a young child and its mother need a safe and warm home, a comfortable bed for the both of them because they will spend many hours sleeping and breastfeeding there, a full fridge, nappies, clothes, a blanket, a baby wrap, a baby bath, and a class on how to massage a sore tummy that's just learning to digest. Although it's hard to believe, when it comes to buying baby things, at the start not much more is needed.

What's essential is social support in the form of your partner, family, friends, a doula, or a psychologist. I would like to strongly emphasise the fact that a young mother has the right to expect this support and help from them.

She has the right to take care of herself and her baby after birth, and for some time abandon all her other roles - that of a lover, an attractive woman, and certainly the role of an employee or the perfect housewife.

During pregnancy, it's already worth preparing yourself for the fact that, despite all those perfect ideas of what your idyllic start to motherhood will be and how wonderfully you'll be looking after your baby, the reality not only may be, but most probably will be quite different.

It's worth realising that, as women, never again in our lives will we be in a situation as demanding and as emotionally challenging as the first time after giving birth.

The great amount of responsibility involved in caring for a child is unimaginable and is also coupled with an enormous amount of stress. The more fear and anxiety a woman feels, and the less support she receives, the greater this stress.

There often comes a time in life when a situation forces us to take care of ourselves, if, of course, no one has taught us to do so beforehand, such as during our childhood. Pregnancy is a good time to think about yourself, what you want your motherhood to be like, what you want your relationship with the baby's father to be like (if the father is present), and even before that, what you want your birth to be like. Pregnancy is a time that is conducive to listening to yourself, and it's worth taking advantage of this time. It is a natural moment when, as women, we feel that a miracle is happening. The fact that a baby is growing in our body, in our uterus, is a miracle. No one consciously monitors this process; we don't know when the egg gets implanted-unless we get implantation bleeding. But in which part of the uterus this happens, that we do not know. We don't know when the embryo becomes the foetus as we don't feel it. It's not like we get a notification on our phones with information on the current state of our baby. We don't know and we don't control when the eyes are formed, we don't plan what colour they will be or when they will open to look at us from the inside. We have no control over any of it.

When you listen to yourself during this time, and when you understand just how very important and yet uncontrollable this whole process is, conflicting feelings may arise. You may feel anxiety related to the lack of control over what is happening. However, this is often also accompanied by a feeling of trust in this force, whatever and whoever this force may be. I will call it nature. Nature, therefore, knows what it's doing. Sometimes it makes mistakes - yes, it happens - however, more often than not, when it decides to create a new human being, it takes control of it effortlessly and confidently. We accept it as if it were the most ordinary thing in the world, and we don't think about how unbelievable and complicated the process is.

From this experience comes a very important lesson – namely, a lesson in trust. Trust in nature, in yourself, and in your body. Trust that your body can give birth naturally and out of nature, and that it can also feed naturally.

A quick survival and psychological self-help guide for future mothers-to-be:

- From the moment that you see those two lines on a test, **don't try to do everything** at home by yourself
- **Don't listen to unwanted advice**, firmly state that you don't want it
- If you want advice, **turn to experienced mothers you know you can trust, or to experts** in the field.
- **Don't look at pictures of perfect 'Fit Mamas'** on Instagram - never!
- Imagine giving birth, draw it, and **make a birth plan**
- **Don't let go of your hobbies**
- **Warn your family and friends** that they are welcome to come over after you've had your baby, but that they shouldn't expect any tea, coffee or biscuits

offered. Rather, it should be you expecting them to bring food, do the washing up or look after the baby so you can go have a shower

- **If you have problems with your emotions, talk it out with your bestie**
- **If that doesn't help, feel free to contact me.** My contact details can be found at the end of this book.

A space for your thoughts and reflections.

AGNIESZKA PLUTA-SZKARADEK

---

1. It should be added that colic results from the fact that the newborn's digestive system is not yet fully developed. It's the result of an irritation to the thin walls and membrane of the intestine, which is only just learning to digest. Before deciding to use magical colic drops, consider whether it's really worth irritating this delicate system even more. Warm compresses, cherry seed compresses and massages are much better. (A. Pluta-Szkaradek)

Acknowledgments

Thank you Grzegorz, my beloved husband, for simply being always there. Like a true doula, he accompanies me during the birth of the new woman within me. Whenever I would leave for work (whether that be as a doula for a birth, or for my book), I knew the house would function normally because of you. Thank you for patiently putting up with my little mood swings and for continuing to adjust your work holidays, trips, and football matches to work around my work schedule and dates. Thank you for the fact that when I have to travel far, you travel with me so that you can drive on the way back, while I sleep soundly in the seat next to you. Thank you for sometimes telling me "NO" when you can see me trying to take on too much and things start taking a negative toll on my physical and mental health. Thank you for watching over and keeping an eye on things that don't always interest you, but you know how much they mean to me. And although it sounds infantile and cliché, I love you to the moon and back.

My dear Natalia, my beloved daughter, when I felt your movements in my belly for the first time, it never even crossed my mind that you could be born in any other way. After all, "everyone" gives birth in a hospital, and so I went there too. Thank you for this experience. Thank you for teaching me every day how to be a better mum. Thank you also for being my doula during Patrycja's birth.

Kacper, your birth made me realise what I don't

want. Thank you for this difficult, but equally enlightening learning experience. I'm sorry that I wasn't strong and independent enough to bring you into this world on my own terms. I am sorry that I did not seek help to breastfeed you. Thank you for your every smile and the endless amounts of cuddles. Remember that you are a very special boy with a tremendous amount of self-awareness. Make the most of what you have and keep smiling at people.

Patrycja, my dear daughter, thank you for bringing the magic back to childbirth for me and for allowing me to experience the miracle of childbirth at home.

Karoline Gorol, thank you for the meeting that only had to last a few seconds for me to realise that you'll change my life forever. Thank you for showing me a fresh, new perspective on midwifery. Thank you for making the Birthing School Instructor classes in Warsaw an amazing time.

Łukasz Jop, first and foremost, I would like to thank you for always blessing us with your smile every time we meet. Your optimism spreads to the people around you and beautifully supports dreams. It is thanks to you that we have once and for all closed the nursery and let go of all the associated feelings of regret, despair, shame, and guilt. While it was certainly a learning experience for me, it nearly led to the break-up of my marriage. Thank you for always believing in us and seeing our love.

Marysia Block, you wonderful woman. It's thanks to you that something which was once just a theory to me was brought to life. Thank you for showing me that childbirth can be a beautiful experience. Thank you for all your words of support and understanding. Thank you also for the fact that even after the birth we've kept in touch, and I was not "just another client". The friendship that developed between us helped me to believe that women need other women to be fully happy. I would also like to thank you for the *Krąg Opowieści o Stracie* meeting, which allowed me to share my miscarriage story with others. Thank you for the tears, for translating the poem about our Charek, and for showing me the value of life. You are and will always be a very special and inspiring woman in my life who I wish to be like.

Monika Grzegorzewska, you beautiful woman. Without you this book would not exist. Although I started writing it before we met, it was thanks to you that it came out. Thank you for constantly motivating me and for keeping an eye on my brain which would quite often be all over the place whenever I would do a hundred thousand things at once. Thank you for being there and for taking care of the part of the job that I don't have a clue about. You're my virtual IT angel.

Magda Bęben. When I first wrote to you, I had no idea that we would start working together so quickly. The illustrations you make bring new ideas to my head faster than a rocket can take off. Thanks to your involvement, this book got a new life and a front cover.

Olga Barbara Pietrzak. I don't know why found yourself on my life's path, but apparently it had to happen. Thank you for all the effort you put into getting this book published. Thank you for becoming a part of it by writing an extract. I trust that your motherhood journey will be positive from the very beginning, and that future generations will not have to heal from emotional wounds and scars.

Agnieszka Michalska. We met in professional circumstances. I came to you first when you needed my help. I felt something extraordinary then, something I had never felt with any client before, and that's how you went from being a client to being my friend. Thank you for all that you have contributed to the development of the *Polska Szkoła Rodzenia w UK* (Polish Birthing

School in the UK) not only in the professional sense, but also for all that you bring into my private life.

I would also like to thank all those women whom I have accompanied so far. Thank you for the trust you place in me and for inviting me to be with you during the most intimate moment in your lives. Thank you for letting me accompany you on your journey to becoming an even stronger woman.

I thank God for the strength, for the peace in my heart that he gave me during my last birth, and for the opportunity to experience childbirth just as I wanted- in the rhythm that my baby and my body set, in the incredible warmth and safety of my own home, with my wonderful husband, my children and my doula Marysia.

Thank you for reading this book. I wish for you all to trust mother nature, your own intuition, your body, as well as your maternal and paternal instincts. I wish for you to have the courage to take responsibility for the birth of your child. May you be able to take birth into your own hands and decide where you want to give birth to your children.

About the Author

AGNIESZKA PLUTA-SZKARADEK

A woman, wife, mum, and doula. She's fascinated by other women and their birthing powers, the incredible bonds they create, and their internal instinct for being a mother. She obtained her master's degree from the University of Silesia in Katowice. She's also completed numerous antenatal courses.

She was trained by Katy Hemus to be the best doula she possibly could be. She continues to expand her knowledge by studying books on pregnancy, childbirth, and the postnatal and postpartum period. She accompanies women during the intimate moment of the birth of their children and works as a non-medical lactation consultant.

She trusts the unborn child and their mother's feminine power to give birth. Her personal experiences allow her to understand the fear of childbirth but also how to move past it. In her career, she strives for every woman to be able to give birth with dignity and in a way that's true to their wants and needs.

Agnieszka Pluta-Szkaradek leads the *Polska Szkoła Rodzenia w UK* (Polish Birthing School in the UK) so that women can prepare for childbirth as best as they can, because after all, *Labour Begins in the Mind*.

Bibliography

Adamczewska E., Tajemnica Narodzin. Poród lotosowy, Białystok, New Space, 2018.

Anderson M.,Tales ofa midwife. A funny, poignant and heart-warming account of a devoted midwife, Londyn, Headline Publishing Group, 2012.

Antosiewicz I.,Nakarm, naucz i puść wolno, Warszawa, Przytulam.pl, 2020.

Balaskas JI.,Active birth, New York, McGraw-Hill Book Company, 1983.

Bliss L., The Doula's guide to empowering your birth, Eeverly, Harvard Common Press,U.S., 2018.

Borgenicht L., Borgenicht J., Bobas. Instrukcja obsługi. Wskazówki użytkowe, wykrywanie i usuwanie usterek oraz porady serwisowe, tłum. E. Helińska, Poznań, Vesper, 2008

Bradshaw J., Powrót do swego wewnętrznego domu: jak odzyskać i otoczyć opieką swoje wewnętrzne dziecko, tłum. C. Urbański, Konstancin-Jeziorna, Wydawnictwo Medium, 2013.

Brott A., The new father. A dad's guide to the first year, Londyn, Abbeville Press, 2005.

Brown A, The positive Breastfeeding book. Everything you need to feed your baby with confidence, Pinter 8 Martin Lta, Londyn 2019.

CannonsE., Total Fertility.How to understana, optimize and preserveyour fertility,Londyn, Macmillan,2013.

Chołuj I.,Urodzić razem inaturalnie, Mszczonów, Fundacja Źródło Życia, 2017.

Churchill H.,Savage W., Vaginal birth after caesarean. The VBAC Handbook, Londyn, Pinter %Martin Ltd., 2010.

Cooke K, Dzieciozmagania. Z maluchem przez pierwsze 5 lat, tłum. B. Gontarczyk-Krampe, Kraków, Insignis Media, 2010.

Cudowne 9 miesięcy. Rozmowy o tym, jak zatroszczyć się o siebie i dziecko w zgodzie z naturą, red. Mirska-Królikowska D., Maciąg A., Warszawa, Dager, 2019.

De Cruz, H., Your baby, Your birth. Hypnobirthing skills for every birth, Londyn, Penguin Random House, 2018.

Delahaye M.-C.,Zdrowa ciąża, tłum. A Gawecka, Warszawa, Hachette Livre Polska, 20T1.

Dembińska I.,Rodzić można łatwiej, Warszawa, Oficyna 4eM, 2019. Dick-Reaad, G., Childbirth without fear, Londyn, Pollinger in Print, 2006.

Bibliography

Dillow L.,Twórcza partnerka: bądź żoną pełną pasji!, tłum. E. Kopocz, Ustroń, Koinonia, 2013.

Domowe narodziny. Fanaberia szaleńców czy powrót do normalności?, red.Janiuk E, Lichtenberg- Kokoszka E.,Kraków,Oficyna Wydawnicza Impuls, 2010.

Dowshen S. A, Izenberg N., Bass E., Dziecko. Zdrowie i rozwój od poczęcia do 5 roku życia, tłum. I. Józefowicz-Pacuła, Warszawa, Świat Książki, 2003.

Dziecko aktywny uczestnik porodu. Zagadnienie interdyscyplinarne, red. Lichtenberg- Kokoszka E.,Janiuk E., Dzierżanowski I., Kraków, Impuls, 2010.

Ermpatia: wzmacnia dzieci, trzyma cały świat razem, red. I. Juul, H. Jensen, P. Hoeg, Podkówka Leśna, Wydawnictwo MiND, 2018.

Escobar M., Kołysanka z Auschwitz, tłum. P. Zarawska, Białystok, Wydawnictwo Kobiece 2019.

Faber A., Mazlish E.,Jak być rodzicem, jakim zawsze chciałeś być, tłum. K. Puławski, Poznań, Media Rodzina, 2015.

Faber A., Mazlish E.,Jak mówić, żeby dzieci nas słuchały. Jak słuchać, żeby dzieci do nas mówiły, tłum. M.Więznowska, B. Horosiewicz, Poznań, Media Rodzinna, 2013.

Faber A., Mazlish E.,Rodzeństwo be rywalizacji. Jak pomóc własnym dzieciom żyć wzgodzie, by samemu żyć z godnością, tłum. B. Horosiewicz, Poznań, Media Rodzinna, 2017.

Faber A., Mazlish E., Wyzwoleni rodzice, wyzwolone dzieci. Twoja droga do szczęśliwszej rodziny, tłum. B. Horosiewicz, Poznań, Media Rodzinna, 2017,

Faber I., King J.,Jak mówić, żeby maluchy nas słuchały: poradnik prze- trwania dla rodziców dzieci w wieku 2-7 lat, Poznań, Media Rodzinna, 2017

Faber J., Mazlish E.,Jak mówić do nastolatków, żeby nas słuchały. Jak słuchać, żebyz nami rozmawiały, tłum. B. Horosiewicz, Poznań, Media Rodzinna, 2016.

Fijałkowski W., Szkoła rodzenia, Warszawa, Państwowy Zakład Wydawnictw Lekarskich, 1974.

FijałkowskiW., Rodzi się człowiek, Warszawa, Państwowy Zakład Wydawnictw Lekarskich, 1977.

Gaskin I.,M.,Karmienie piersią,tłum. K.Bogdan, Warszawa,CoJaNaTo,2012.

Giles, S.,Jestem tatą: od pieluszkowego bałaganu do szczęścia: sztuka bycia wspaniałym tatą, tłum. M.Gołębiowska, Warszawa, Oficyna Wydawniczo- Poligraficzna „Adam", 2007.

Guzik A, Guzik B., Komunikacja w małżeństwie i w rodzinie, Kraków, Wydawnictwo Światło-Życie, 2010

Hansard K. The Secrets od Birth. What every woman needs to know about birth and motherhood, Południowa Karolina, CreateSpace Independent Publishing Platform, 2015.

Hazard L.,Hard pushed, A midwife's story, Londyn, Cornerstone Digital, 2019

Bibliography

Hearn I.,Birth and afterbirth.A Materialist Account, Londyn, Achilles Heel, 1983.
Hill M.,The Positive Birth book. A new approach to pregnancy, birth and the early weeks, Londyn, Pinter and Martin, 2017.
Hul M.,Osadnik K.,Cesarskie cięcie iporód po cięciu cesarskim, Szczecin, Natuli, 2020.
Juul I, Zamiast wychowania. O sile relacji z dzieckiem, tłum. D. Syska, Podkowa Leśna: Wydawnictwo MiND, 2016.
Kalyta I., Położna. 3550 cudów narodzin, Kraków,Wydawnictwo Otwarte,2014.
McCarthy S., (Dlaczego) macierzyństwo jest cenne, tłum. M. Zubrycka- -Wernerowska, Cieszyn, Wydawnictwo Zacheusz, 2018.
Minge N.,Minge K. Rodzicielstwo bliskości.Jak zbudować więź z dzieckierm,Warszawa,Edgard, 2013.
Mize J, Cud narodzin. Poznaj Boga, dla którego żadna rzecz nie jest niemożliwa, tłum. J. Kaniewska, Ustroń, Koinonia Wydawnictwo
Chrześcijańskiej Fundacji Życie i Misja, 2015.
Murkoff, H., Mazel, S., Pierwszy rok życia dziecka, tłum. M.Hermanowska, Poznań, Dom Wydawniczy Rebis, 2017.
Murkoff, H.,Mazel, S., Woczekiwaniu na dziecko. Najlepszy poradnik dla przyszłych matek i ojców, tłum. M.Rozwarzewska, Poznań, Dom Wydawniczy Rebis, 2011.
Jak zrozumieć małe dziecko, Nuckowska A.,Krogulska E.,Siudut-Stajura A. iin., Szczecin, Natuli,2019.
Odent M, Do we need midwifes?, Londyr, Pinter et Martin, 2015.
Odent M, Primal health. Understanding the critical period between conception and the first birthday, La Vergne, Rudolf Steiner Press, 20T2.
Odent M.,Woter and sexuolity, Londyn, Arkana, 1990.
Odent M. The Caesarean, Londyn, Free Association Books, 2004.
Odent M. Odrodzone narodziny: jak powinny rodzić się dzieci, tłum. H.Jankowska, Krosno, Dom Wydawniczy Bela Med.,2009.
Oleś K, Poród naturalny, Szczecin, Natuli,2018.
Piotrowska K.,Błogosławiony stan umysłu. Bajki terapeutyczne dla kobiet wciąży, Białystok,Vivante,2016.
Piotrowska K., Rozwój seksualny dzieci, Rybna, Natuli, 2020, Powideł A., Cesarzowa rodzi w domu, Łódź, Filome, 2019.
Reid J., Williams E., Być wciąży i (nie)*zwariować. Antyporadnik dla przyszłych rodziców, tłum. A. Celińska, Warszawa, Buchmann, 2018.
Renaud G. PRecallHealing. Totalna Biologia. Leksykon, tłum. A. Laskowska, M.Witalewski, Poznań, Wydawnictwo WENA Studio Twórczej Ekspresji, 2014.

Bibliography

Schutzenberger A.A.,Psychogeneoalogiawpraktyce, tłum. B.Łyszkowska, Warszawa,Virgo,2017,

McCarthy S., (Dlaczego) macierzyństwo jest cenne, tłum. M. Zubrycka-Wernerowska, Cieszyn, Wydawnictwo Zacheusz, 2018.

Minge N.,Minge K. Rodzicielstwo bliskości.Jak zbudować więź z dzieckierm,Warszawa,Edgard, 2013.

Mize J, Cud narodzin. Poznaj Boga, dla którego żadna rzecz nie jest niemożliwa, tłum. J. Kaniewska, Ustroń, Koinonia Wydawnictwo Chrześcijańskiej Fundacji Życie i Misja, 2015.

Murkoff, H., Mazel, S., Pierwszy rok życia dziecka, tłum. M.Hermanowska, Poznań, Dom Wydawniczy Rebis, 2017.

Murkoff, H.,Mazel, S., Woczekiwaniu na dziecko. Najlepszy poradnik dla przyszłych matek i ojców, tłum. M.Rozwarzewska, Poznań, Dom Wydawniczy Rebis, 2011.

Jak zrozumieć małe dziecko, Nuckowska A.,Krogulska E.,Siudut-Stajura A. iin., Szczecin, Natuli,2019.

Odent M, Do we need midwifes?, Londyr, Pinter et Martin, 2015.

Odent M, Primal health. Understanding the critical period between conception and the first birthday, La Vergne, Rudolf Steiner Press, 20T2.

Odent M.,Woter and sexuality, Londyn, Arkana, 1990.

Odent M. The Caesarean, Londyn, Free Association Books, 2004.

Odent M. Odrodzone narodziny: jak powinny rodzić się dzieci, tłum. H.Jankowska, Krosno, Dom Wydawniczy Bela Med.,2009.

Oleś K, Poród naturalny, Szczecin, Natuli,2018.

Piotrowska K.,Błogosławiony stan umysłu. Bajki terapeutyczne dla kobiet wciąży, Białystok,Vivante,2016.

Piotrowska K., Rozwój seksualny dzieci, Rybna, Natuli, 2020, Powideł A., Cesarzowa rodzi w domu, Łódź, Filome, 2019.

Reid J., Williams E., Być wciąży i (nie)*zwariować. Antyporadnik dla przyszłych rodziców, tłum. A. Celińska, Warszawa, Buchmann, 2018.

Renaud G. PRecallHealing. Totalna Biologia. Leksykon, tłum. A. Laskowska, M.Witalewski, Poznań, Wydawnictwo WENA Studio Twórczej Ekspresji, 2014.

Schutzenberger A.A.,Psychogeneoalogiawpraktyce, tłum. B.Łyszkowska, Warszawa,Virgo,2017,

Become A Doula!

Join us at the Polish Birthing School and embark on an exciting journey together! We are thrilled to offer you a range of specialized classes designed to help you prepare for childbirth, postpartum care, and breastfeeding.

Our workshops are in polish led by a team of highly qualified professionals who are passionate about supporting you every step of the way. Our team includes experienced doula educators, skilled midwives, caring psychologists, expert urogynecological physiotherapists, and certified breastfeeding consultants.

Stay connected with us on social media for updates and inspiration. If you have any questions or need more information, feel free to send us an email. We can't wait to be part of your incredible birthing experience!

https://www.subscribepage.com/kursdoula

Open Polish Birthing School in Your Area!

Attention Doulas, Midwives, and Birth Professionals!

Are you a passionate birth professional, doula, or midwife seeking a rewarding opportunity to make a positive impact on families during their childbirth journey? Open Polish Birthing School!

As an esteemed member of our birthing school, you'll have the opportunity to share your expertise, knowledge, and skills with a diverse community of expectant parents. **Together, we can empower individuals and couples to make informed choices and have positive birth experiences.**

At the Polish Birthing School, we value collaboration and believe in a holistic approach to childbirth education. We offer a comprehensive curriculum that covers prenatal care, labor and delivery techniques, postpartum support, and newborn care. Your valuable contributions will help shape our classes, ensuring they are informative, engaging, and tailored to meet the needs of our participants.

Joining our team means being part of a supportive network of birth professionals who are passionate about making a difference. Together, we can create a warm and inclusive environment where expectant parents can access the guidance and support they need during this transformative time in their lives.

Don't miss this incredible opportunity to be at the forefront of childbirth education in your area. **Join the Polish Birthing School and play a vital role in empowering polish speaking parents and promoting positive birth experiences.**

For more information and to express your interest, please visit our website or contact us using the details below:

Website: www.polskaszkolarodzenia.co.uk
Email: animator.office@gmail.com
Phone: +44 7401203737

Open Polish Birthing School - Empowering Birth Professionals, Celebrating Birth!

Printed in Great Britain
by Amazon